The Children's Media Yearbook is a publication of The Children's Media Foundation

Director, Greg Childs
Administrator, Jacqui Wells

The Children's Media Foundation
15 Briarbank Rd
London
W13 0HH

info@thechildrensmediafoundation.org

First published 2021

ISBN 978-1-9161353-4-5

Book design by Camilla Umar

The Children's Media
FOUNDATION

CHILDREN'S MEDIA YEARBOOK 2021

The Children's Media Conference is the annual gathering of professionals engaged in communicating to and entertaining kids and young people in the UK, Ireland and beyond. CMC is proud to support this year's Children's Media Yearbook and to be able to distribute it to all our CMC 2021 Online delegates.

THE CHILDREN'S MEDIA CONFERENCE
5–9 JULY 2021
ONLINE

Together

HOLD THE FRONT PAGE!

Exclusive! Children's Media Foundation has the important stories that have shaped children's media this year.

CMF YEARBOOK EDITORIAL:

One Year On: What's Changed?

DIANA HINSHELWOOD

Editor, Children's Media Yearbook 2021

I don't think I need to say what a strange year this has been. But I'll say it anyway.

So many changes; some good – time at home, learning new skills, rediscovering nature, and some not so good, particularly for young people – not seeing friends and family, home schooling, and uncertainty over exams.

Despite all that, there are wonderful stories of perseverance and success. The children's media industry has continued to produce excellent content by adapting to restrictions and social distancing. Digital education providers, led by BBC Bitesize and BBC Learning, have upped their game in home schooling. The gaming phenomenon has been extraordinary, and the result is not the usual cliché of isolated teens. And it's also good to see books enjoying a huge surge in popularity amongst the young when screen time has come to dominate their lives.

As we noted in last year's Yearbook, children are far more accepting of difference than previous generations, and diversity and inclusion is important to them. But simply putting diverse groups on screen isn't enough and representation is emerging as the key to audiences recognising themselves.

In most of this year's articles mental health has emerged either as a major theme or a thread in the consequence of lockdowns. Producer Sallyann Keizer has written a heartfelt piece about children's mental health and the need to provide content to address them.

Other issues this year include the slow progress towards online regulation and the elimination of online harms. Articles focused on the internet include Baroness Beeban Kidron, OBE, outlining the successful campaign to include digital rights in the UN's treaty on the Rights of the Child.

The future of public service broadcasting, updated to public service media in the latest Ofcom report, features in CMF Deputy Director Colin Ward's article which recommends we read the Yearbook's "sister

THE CHILDREN'S MEDIA CONFERENCE

publication" for 2021 – the CMF Report: "Our Children's Future – Does Public Service Media Matter?"

CMF will be debating the future of public service media at the Children's Media Conference, which is online again this year, as is Yearbook 2021. It seems that despite the strangeness of the year, there's no need to miss out on the discussions and issues that have occupied us.

Thank you to all the contributors who wrote for this book. The articles highlight the wide range of issues facing children's media, and the high level of expertise, insight and creativity evident in the success and resilience of the industry that serves children and young people with their media choices.

All achieved in the most difficult circumstances, despite these strange times. Amazing! ◔

Diana

THE ISSUES AHEAD

ANNA HOME OBE

Chair, the Children's Media Foundation

—

This time last year, in May 2020, we were already aware that Covid would have a considerable impact on the media world, but we had no idea of what the scale of that impact would be; on jobs, on production, on audiences and, in particular, on children's media which was already changing in terms of viewing habits and loyalties.

Covid brought home working and home learning, Zoom, and a huge rise in media consumption, especially online for those who had access. Sadly, many children didn't, but the Public Service Broadcasters - particularly the BBC - responded quickly by providing increased educational content on the linear channels.

These changes have made creators, broadcasters, regulators, educators and politicians, reassess the whole structure of media in the UK and worldwide.

Future thinking had already started in July 2019 when Ofcom launched the first phase of its public service inquiry *Small Screen: Big Debate*, followed by a public consultation in December which closed in March this year.

The tone of this consultation was much more forward-looking and radical than previously, and this has been reflected in many of the debates and conferences on the future of Public Service Broadcasting which have gone on during the year. The impact of Covid on society, and the reaction of the PSB broadcasters, particularly the BBC, has highlighted their value to the public, and especially to children in terms of education and information. There seems to be a general consensus, for the moment at least, that public service channels are a "good thing".

However, the problems for the PSBs around funding remain, with the licence fee for the BBC in question, and decreasing advertising revenue for the commercial PSBs. Added to which, migrating audiences, particularly among young people, increase the need for thinking about new issues like prominence.

Ofcom's public service recommendations will be published this summer and are certain to be hotly debated.

The Children's Media FOUNDATION

There are many questions to be answered...

How long can the traditional structures of PSB survive? Should they? Or are there new ways to deliver and fund PSB/ PSM content? Where do we go from here to maintain public service media in the future? These are all questions we in Children's Media Foundation have been asking ourselves.

The Ofcom consultation, which CMF responded to, did not have a lot to say about children, so we have gone ahead with our own project which I mentioned last year, to investigate ways forward for children's public service content in the future, through a series of commissioned essays now available on our website to be followed by a report presented at The Children's Media Conference.

Colin Ward who is editing the project will describe it in much more detail in his article for this yearbook.

THE CHILDREN'S MEDIA CONFERENCE
5-9 JULY 2021 ONLINE

Central to the future of PSM for UK children remains the BBC which is currently under continuing funding pressure, despite its Covid successes. The Children's area is no exception to these cuts, and they are starting to impact on the output. The structure of BBC Children's is also going to change radically from next year when the production arm moves into BBC Studios. This may well bring benefits in terms of additional funding and greater flexibility, but there may also be dangers. CMF has an open mind at present but will be keeping a close watch on how things develop. This change was revealed shortly after news of the implications of the return of BBC Three to television, with the result that the early evening hours of airtime CBBC inherited from BBC Three's closure as a channel some years ago, have now been re-allocated to BBC Three with the aim of offering content targeted at 13 to 15 year olds, bridging the gap between children's programmes and the BBC 3 target audience. We welcome the provision of content for this underserved audience and hope to see some new and original programming as a result.

Last year I referred to the Government's Online Harms bill as being in Limbo. Sadly, it has remained there - ostensibly as a result of Covid.

This bill will give Ofcom considerable powers to fine online providers that fail to protect under 18 audiences from access to a wide range of inappropriate content including pornography, trolling, and other harmful content.

New Online Harms Laws
#SafeOnline

This bill was included in this year's Queen's Speech. It is therefore unlikely to become law before 2023/24. CMF deplores this delay. Especially in the aftermath of Covid, when children are particularly vulnerable.

We feel the same concern about the lack of action in the area of children's online gambling through the use of loot boxes. We will continue to argue for more progress on this issue in the coming year.

**Department for
Digital, Culture
Media & Sport**

However, there has been much more positive news in one area. Despite the difficulties due to Covid, the Young Audiences Content Fund (the YAC Fund) has made excellent progress. It has achieved its targets, enabling a range of broadcasters to commission a diverse series of productions from a wide variety of companies, established and new. The Fund is clearly already making a welcome impact on the market.

However there was a sudden setback towards the end of May when the DCMS announced a 25% cut to the fund's final year budget, and there were rumours that the future of the fund might in some way become part of the upcoming BBC licence fee negotiations.

CMF believes that the fund is very important for the long-term future of Children's PSM, that it should be adequately funded, and that it should not be financed by further erosion of the BBC licence fee but by exploring alternative new funding possibilities and partnerships.

We await further developments and trust that this exciting new initiative will be allowed to develop and flourish as it deserves to the benefit of all children in the UK. ○

THE FOUNDATION LOOKS TO THE FUTURE

GREG CHILDS

Director, The Children's Media Foundation

It says something about the times we live in that my article for the Yearbook last summer, started with the phrase "as we come out of lockdown". Here we go again. Perhaps with more to be optimistic about than a year ago, but also chastened by the tragic loss of life, the long-term implications of Covid infection, the incredible dedication of so many in the health and care services and other key workers, and the way children and young people have been affected by the disruption, worry, and economic and educational uncertainty.

The accelerated changes that happened in society and in individuals' choices and habits over the last 16 months are seen by many as an opportunity to re-set priorities and rebuild with fresh eyes and new agendas. It remains to be seen how that will turn out in the long-term. One thing we can be fairly sure of is that young people, for whom a year-and-a-half represents a significant chunk of their lived experience, living through "the time of Covid" will leave a lasting impact on their mental well-being, attitudes and expectations. Talking to people in the media industry who talk to kids and teens on a regular basis, my sense of the future is one in which #metoo and BLM will become templates for uncompromising action amongst the young. The buzzwords for media makers and content distributors in the future will, I believe, be *listening, involving, empowerment, embracing activism* and *supporting change*. Change that many young people see as long overdue - in the hands of a generation that has failed to secure the future for its young people.

The Children's Media Foundation has devoted much of its time and effort in the last year to preparing, and now rolling out, our consideration of possible futures. Our Public Service Content Campaign – brilliantly driven by CMF Deputy Director Colin Ward with help from a small team of volunteers from our Executive Working Group has produced a series of articles which are essentially the only conversation taking place now about the future of content for young people. They investigate what public service means for the younger audience, why it's important to society as a whole, how the young are deserting the traditional outlets and what the implications might be for a variety of

possible future plans for delivering meaningful, free content to young people that connects them to the society in which they live and its many and varied cultures.

We are thrilled that figures as eminent and experienced as their Lordships **Vaizey** and **Puttnam**, **Phil Redmond, Frank Cottrell-Boyce,** and a range of academic and journalist contributors have offered their thoughts on various aspects of the future of public service media. And I thoroughly recommend the final compilation of articles in the report which, like this Yearbook, are available as a digital download.

People of note in the children's media industry have also come forward this year in support of CMF itself. New lifetime patrons Keith Chapman and Tom Van Waveren have given generous financial support as well as access to years of experience in the animation sector. Wincie Knight VP of Global Inclusion Strategies at ViacomCBS Networks International has joined the CMF Board, contributing a wealth of experience in inclusion strategies in the broadcast sector. Alison Stewart, former Head of Production for CBeebies, has

also joined the Board and the CMF Executive Group, our volunteer force carrying out much of the work and activity which sustains the organisation and its aims. A number of new people joined this working group during 2020-21. We are hugely grateful to everyone for their commitment.

Funding for the Foundation remains entirely in the hands of donors: supporters, patrons, companies, supporting organisations and our lifetime patrons. We are in their debt and will continue to be watchful on their behalf – and that of the children's and youth audience – keeping ahead of regulatory or policy changes and activities in the market which might have an effect on young people as viewers and users of content.

Through the course of the past year, we have supported various initiatives connected with safety online and the government's Online Safety Bill (originally the Online Harms Bill) which is still in limbo. We publicly backed Baroness Howe's Private Members Bill to try to force the government to enact the online harms legislation it already has in place via Part 3 of the Digital Economies Act. This would have made age-verification mandatory for legal porn websites. Baroness Howe's bill did not succeed, and the government has made that useful piece of legislation quietly fade away.

However, Baroness Kidron's 5Rights Campaign scored a fantastic success when it successfully lobbied the UN to include children's digital rights in the Declaration of the Rights of the Child. Beeban Kidron provides more detail in an article in this Yearbook. It's a historic change which CMF is proud to have supported.

These and the various issues around children's and youth media, some of which are outlined below, are regularly communicated to parliamentarians by Jayne Kirkham who acts as secretary to the All-Party Parliamentary Group for Children's Media and the Arts, chaired by **Baroness Floella Benjamin** and **Julie Elliott MP**. We also communicate with our own supporters and patrons in the monthly CMF newsletter, and of course this Yearbook covers a wide range of topics – creative, research and policy-based – and once again the Yearbook will be distributed to all delegates at the Children's Media Conference in July. CMF Executive Group members involve themselves deeply in the Conference, producing sessions like the annual policy Question Time, and this year a debate on the future of public service content. This is a significant part of our continuing conversation with the children's media industry.

Topics that have particularly concerned us over the course of the last year include Safety Online, the future of public service media and changes at BBC Children's.

Regulation of internet services began in 2020-21. It's something CMF has long felt was overdue, with many suggesting it was impossible to achieve. A variety of disruptions to modern life have combined to make this a hot topic – from fake news and election interference, to concerns about pornography and young people, or about collection of personal data from children and many more.

In September 2020 CMF responded to a consultation on the methods Ofcom will use to regulate user-generated video sharing sites (YouTube and anything similar). This was a frustrating exercise as in reality regulatory powers reside in the country which hosts the head office of the web platform. As a result, YouTube will be regulated from Dublin. Ofcom will regulate smaller platforms based here in the UK.

However, progress is being made. In late 2020 a useful meeting with YouTube clarified a number of questions around new safety measure taken by the platform in recent months. Keeping ahead in understanding the platforms and children's uses of them is a major part of the process for CMF. And discussing our concerns with the platform operators rather than being constantly in "campaign mode" is of much more value in the long run.

Potential changes to public service media began to rise to the surface in April 2020 as the government consulted on de-criminalising licence fee evasion. We responded with concerns about diminishing funding for the BBC and how that would impact on kids' content. The decriminalisation idea has now been rolled forward as part of the 2022-27 licence fee discussions – so the imminent danger of loss of revenue has passed.

By March 2021 the future of public service content in the UK took centre-stage. It was the subject of an Ofcom report – *Small Screen: Big Debate*. And the Parliamentary DCMS select committee produced *The Future of Public Service Broadcasting*, in which the committee concluded that the Government is forced to maintain the licence fee for the time being, because it has failed to put in place broadband infrastructure that would allow for other funding mechanisms (like subscription).

Both these major reports fail to take any significant account of child or teen audiences. In our responses to them we have pointed out that the flexible, technically savvy younger audience – already massively migrated to digital, on demand and social media services – is the key to understanding the future landscape for delivery of public service content. Hence our own Public Service Content Report which we will feed into future government consultations as plans for change are considered.

As we entered 2021, changes were emerging in BBC Children's and Education. The plan to re-establish BBC Three as a television channel, six years after it was made digital only, will impact on the CBBC channel. Under the new proposals, two hours of the channel's airtime (from 7-9pm daily) will be given over to BBC Three. BBC Three has promised to provide programmes in this slot for the 13-15-year-old audience, currently not addressed by CBBC. We welcome a specific younger audience having content aimed at its needs and interests. But we will be watchful that this commitment is real - not a whitewash.

Meanwhile an ambitious plan to move the entire in-house production operation for CBBC and CBeebies to the BBC Studios commercial arm of the Corporation has also been floated as part of the master-plan to make BBC Studios more profitable. For CMF, what's vital is that the special expertise and commitment of dedicated children's programme-makers is not diluted or lost when it becomes part of a larger organisation with an international focus, commercial aims and an eye on the bottom line. Once again, we think this needs a watching brief.

So, as ever this is a report on work in progress. CMF will continue to keep watch for anything affecting the children's media industry's capacity to provide the very best content for kids. And as can be seen from the matters listed above, staying alert and active in advocating for the young audience is still very much needed. Your donations help us achieve this, so please join us as a supporter or patron to help us fight the good fight.

Greg Childs, Director
The Children's Media Foundation

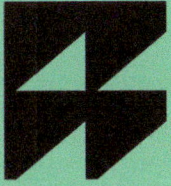

Authors' Licensing and Collecting Society

We believe that the contribution writers make to society should be valued – that's why we campaign to protect copyright, authors' rights and vital revenue streams for creators. No one else in the world does exactly what we do.

The Authors' Licensing and Collecting Society (ALCS) is dedicated to protecting authors' rights and ensuring they are paid for secondary uses of their works. Set up for writers by writers in 1977, since then **we have paid out £570m to our members.**

Whether you're a scriptwriter, a translator, a novelist, an academic writer or a poet, you could be eligible to join 112,000 other members and **start receiving money you're owed for your work.**

Find out more and join online >> **alcs.co.uk**

GREAT EXPECTATIONS

So much has happened since the first lockdown in March 2020, and the issues facing Children's Media are greater than ever. Facilitating change to meet that challenge is a huge task, but we're tackling those issues together. There's been some great successes in children's media rights, even if in the case of online safety, it sometimes it feels like two steps forward and one step back.

Mitch Hodge, Unsplash

WHATEVER HAPPENED TO THE ONLINE HARMS BILL?

BY JAYNE KIRKHAM

Whatever happened to the Online Harms Bill? Don't ask, it's here now. Finally. That promised piece of legislation they said would supersede the part in the Digital Economy Act 2017 (that hard-won part may I say) that protected children from accessing commercial online pornography.

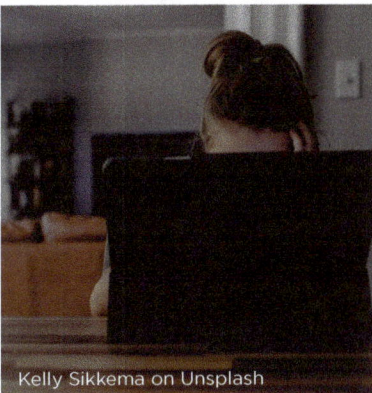
Kelly Sikkema on Unsplash

For those that care about children's vulnerability and are aware of the continued rise of online sexual exploitation, bullying and misinformation, this has been a long four years. Knowing four years is roughly a quarter of a childhood, and knowing that what they experience during that time will colour the rest of their lives, gives this issue an urgency. An urgency that the pandemic, with all of us reliant upon the internet has only intensified. So much so that on 19th November 2020, the House of Commons urged the Government to bring forward the Online Harms Bill as soon as possible, and the Under-Secretary of State for Digital, Culture, Media and Sport acknowledged that the Government must do more to better protect children and adults from online harm.

Well then, has it done more? Six months later, May 2021, the Government has finally published its draft Online Safety Bill.

Introducing the bill, the Secretary of State for Digital, Culture, Media and Sport, Right Hon Oliver Dowden MP said, "This ground-breaking piece of legislation will deliver our manifesto commitment of making the UK the safest place in the world to be online, while also, crucially, protecting freedom of expression."[1]

Yet as soon as anyone had a chance to read the full 145 pages

Right Hon Oliver Dowden MP

---

1 https://hansard.parliament.uk/Commons/2021-05-12/debates/21051242000021/OnlineSafetyBillUpdate

Beeban Kidron

of the Bill, there were criticisms from all sides.

In the Queen' Speech debate in the House of Lords, Baroness Kidron OBE noted the change in the bill's name from 'online harms' to 'online safety'. She said this, "reflects the journey the Bill has been on, and the widespread acceptance that we must stop arguing over what is and is not acceptable after children have suffered harm, and instead seek to tackle risks inherent in the technology they are offered and make it safe from the get-go."[2]

With the title change, the draft bill would seem to be off to a promising start. However, in the same speech, Baroness Kidron went on to say that, "Less welcome is the change of language from the promised 'duty of care' to a list of 'duties of care'. A small grammatical change that could go unnoticed but allowing masses of wriggle room for those who would seek to wriggle out of their responsibilities. As Baroness Kidron said, "We have been promised an end to the 'move fast and break things' culture of the sector, and the Bill must introduce a duty of care as a matter of principle, not a laundry list of pre-circumscribed duties."[3]

Others also had reservations. Highlighting the phrase 'not illegal, but harmful', within the draft Bill, Denise Almeida writing for the Matrix Foundation said, "This puts responsibility on organisations themselves to arbitrarily decide what might be harmful, without any legal backing. The bill itself does not actually provide a definition of harmful, instead relying on service providers to assess and decide on this. This requirement to identify what is 'likely to be harmful' applies to all users, children and adults. Our question here is – would you trust a service provider to decide what might be harmful to you and your children, with zero input from you as a user?"[4]

So, is this just 145 pages of Sir Humphrey-speak? In trying to ensure a free, open and secure internet that is safe for all while protecting freedom of expression, does this Bill in fact fail on all sides? What does it actually say? I waded through it and, I'll be honest, I did get lost in the Sir Humphrey-speak. But as far as I can make out, the draft Bill is a framework Bill, on which to hang large pieces of secondary legislation, codes of practice and government guidance.

Although the Government was keen to play up the world-leading and historic nature of the Bill, with its protection of children, freedom of expression and journalistic content, there is no overarching duty of care. Instead, three separate duties of care, with three partial exemptions from those duties are proposed. Each of these are then dealt with separately for user generated content services and for search engines,

2 https://hansard.parliament.uk/lords/2021-05-18/debates/33A25936-7C04-40A5-8CAD-EB920FB58292/Queen'SSpeech#contribution-2841CC25-6549-4F11-8B72-A2FC10728BAB
3 Ibid.
4 https://matrix.org/blog/2021/05/19/how-the-u-ks-online-safety-bill-threatens-matrix

leading to much repetition and cross referencing. Is this a problem? Is it all too vague?

In her speech in the Lords' debate, Baroness Kidron highlighted that the draft Bill "spends the bulk of its pages on rules that pertain to content - which undermines the stated ambition to tackle risk at a systemic level, as it leaves only cursory mention of the algorithms, functionalities and operating practices that drive user experience."[5] Hardly the 'Safer By Design' idea that the Children's Media Foundation and organisations such as 5Rights called for.

Other concerns raised include the failure to address cross-platform abuse,[6] whether the Bill will be able to keep up with fast-evolving technology[7] and whether Ofcom, as the regulator will have strong enough powers[8].

Those more interested in the other aspects of the draft Bill, free speech for example, are also critical. Mark Glendenning from the Institute for Economic Affairs said: "The proposed Online Safety Bill operates according to such a broad definition of what constitutes harm that virtually anything could end up being taken down by the regulator because it might offend or induce anxiety in some individuals. Why can't adults not simply be left to decide for themselves what they view and make up their own minds concerning what is nonsense and what has validity?"[9]

I guess the answer to that is there in the Secretary of State's introduction to the bill, that the strongest provisions in the legislation are for children: "all companies in scope of this legislation will need to consider the risks that their sites may pose to the youngest and most vulnerable members of society."[10]

But are the youngest and most vulnerable considered really? John Carr, from the Children's Charities Coalition on Internet Safety says, "As currently drafted, the Online Safety Bill applies only to sites or services which allow user interactivity. … However, some of the 'most visited pornography sites' either already do not allow user interactivity or they could easily escape the clutches of legislation written that way simply by disallowing it in the future. That would not affect their core business model in any significant way, if at all."[11]

In 2017, we had some protection for the youngest and most vulnerable members of society in that tiny but hard-won amendment to the Digital Economy Act that insisted on Age Verification of users of these 'most visited pornography sites.' Now we have the draft Bill promised to

---

5 https://hansard.parliament.uk/lords/2021-05-18/debates/33A25936-7C04-40A5-8CAD-EB920FB58292/Queen'SSpeech#contribution-2841CC25-6549-4F11-8B72-A2FC10728BAB
6 NSPCC
7 https://www.catch-22.org.uk/news/catch22-responds-draft-online-safety-bill/
8 https://parentzone.org.uk/article/online-safety-bill-and-what-it-really-means
9 https://iea.org.uk/on-free-speech-the-queens-speech-was-a-mixed-bag/
10 https://hansard.parliament.uk/Commons/2021-05-12/debates/21051242000021/OnlineSafetyBillUpdate
11 https://johncarr.blog/2021/05/15/government-in-a-muddle-over-porn/

Julie Elliott MP

supersede it. Yet despite all its bells and whistles, it fails to give any of the protection provided by that amendment. Fortunately, Co-chair of the All-Party Parliamentary Group for Children's Media and the Arts, Julie Elliott MP was quickly on the case, asking the Secretary of State, when he appeared before the DCMS Select Committee, why commercial pornography sites had been omitted from the scope of the Bill. Mr Dowden's reply suggested he would accept an amendment during pre-legislative scrutiny: "That is one bauble I might be open to hanging on the Christmas tree."[12]

Despite the apparent flippancy of the remark, it is good to know that the Government is open to suggestion. A Joint Scrutiny Committee is to be appointed. Then pre-legislative scrutiny will last for 12 weeks, although there will be a pause for summer recess during that time. This will be a critical time for anyone interested in online safety and freedoms. No doubt those that want plenty of wriggle room will lobby hard but child safety should not be open to interpretation. As of 4th February 2021, The United Nations Convention on the Rights of the Child now gives children the same rights online as offline. We have the opportunity now, to put our young people's best interests at the heart of this legislation. And we should. It will take a further 4 years to get this draft Bill finally on the statute book. That's another quarter of a childhood. As the APPG for Children's Media and the Arts fellow co-chair Baroness Floella Benjamin OBE DL says, "Childhood lasts a lifetime." The Online Safety Bill needs to get it right. ◯

---

12 https://bit.ly/3guFpRN

AT THE MERCY OF THE MARKET – WHAT NEXT FOR THE CHILDREN'S AUDIENCE?

COLIN WARD

—

The UK has a long tradition of regulated public service broadcasting. For many years, the BBC and ITV controlled children's media experiences, feeding them a balanced diet of age-appropriate animation, live action drama, entertainment and factual programming. Even when the cabsats arrived on the scene in the late 1980's and early 90s, it was still the PSBs that dominated children's experiences.

And of course, back in the day, we were given only so much TV and no more. We were forced, often reluctantly, to watch whatever was on the box when kids' programmes ended, which usually meant local and national news.

Back then, children were at the mercy of a bunch of well-meaning, University educated, (largely) middle class producers, who were passionate about the audience and loved telling them stories. That may be an over-generalisation, but it's not far from the truth. Sometimes that eclectic mix of producers and directors delivered amazing, ground-breaking shows and sometimes they got it spectacularly wrong. It wasn't perfect, but what it did have was a strong culture of care for the audience and a commitment to understanding children's needs. Today, even the phrase 'age-appropriate' is beginning to sound like an anachronism. Who cares if it's age-appropriate? Does it get 'likes'? Does it get shared? Does it get more users signing up? Kids are now at the mercy of the market.

And that, of course, is an equally unfair generalisation. We know there are many producers and executives working for commercial children's media companies who are passionate about the children's audience and care deeply about their safety and well-being. Many of them started their careers at a PSB, so their instinct will always be to debate and question what is best for the children's audience.

And yet… it feels as though something is being lost. Something is being forgotten. And sometimes it seems like that is all we are doing - debating. We debate, we question, and meanwhile the media experiences of children have changed dramatically and out of all recognition, with the direction of change determined, largely, by the goals and the needs of a group of very large, global media businesses.

That was the conclusion we reached at a CMF meeting back in January 2020. We were, once again, debating. We were going over the same issues we'd been focused on for ten years. How could we help to persuade ITV, Five and Channel Four to put a little more money into the shows they had started to commission through the Young Audiences Content fund? How could we help BBC Children's defend or even increase their budget with the BBC facing overall budget cuts? What was the best way to engage with YouTube, the most popular media content provider for children, and persuade them to offer more than just support for age-appropriate content for 'national' audiences, as well as giving serious consideration to their responsibility for making the YouTube experience 100% safe for children? And how could we best support the UK's children's production sector to ensure we would, as a nation, continue to have the capacity to tell culturally-relevant stories to our children through their media experiences?

Those questions are all valid and important, but we had the feeling that answering them, and even taking action on those issues, was no longer going to be enough. It is a cliché, but the truth is we were playing the same tune on the fiddle and Rome was burning. More was needed. More had to be done.

And that was the start of the Children's Media Foundation's Public Service Media campaign. We have one overarching goal; to force Ofcom and the government to put the children's audience right at the very centre of the coming national debate on the future of public service broadcasting. Before the next general election, the government is going to legislate for a new PSM framework that will try to determine the future of public service media for a generation. And, at the moment, the children's audience is barely even mentioned in this process.

It was Professor Jeanette Steemers, a member of the CMF's Academic Advisory Board, who first made this point about the tendency to ignore children in a public service review. She proposed we launch a parallel inquiry into public service media that focused on the needs of the children's audience. Ofcom had started its 'Small Screen, Big Debate' consultations and we were already responding to that, but we wanted to do more.

There are limits to what we can take on. But one thing we are very good at is persuading people to help out when the bandits are stealing our crops. We brought in The Magnificent Seven, which actually turned out to be the Magnificent Twenty-Five. A collection of writers, academics, policymakers and producers prepared to give of their time, experience and talent to create articles for a report on the future of public service media for children. That report is being launched at the Children's Media Conference 2021 in July and is a free download for all delegates.

One of the basic aims of the CMF is to raise the quality of the debate around children's media. In the report, we have brilliant articles from a wide range of authors, including **Frank Cottrell-Boyce, Emerita Professor Maire Messenger-Davies, Sir Phil Redmond, Wincie Knight, Lord Puttnam, Anne Wood Jackie Edwards**, and **Lord Vaizey**. Please have a read. Just dip into one or two of them and I guarantee you will find something provocative to consider.

The report will be shared with politicians and policymakers and we will use the ideas contained in the articles to frame our lobbying of Ofcom and the government. There will also be a series of online events in the autumn to keep up the pressure and develop our arguments. We hope you will be able to attend and lend your support to this campaign.

Of course, there is a question to be asked; why should the children's audience be at the very centre of this national debate? Is public service media for children really more important than what happens to news services or the future of UK-originated, high-end drama? Well, it is. Fifteen years ago we told ITV they were crazy to pull out of children's programming, because once you lose an audience, they don't come back. Now, in 2021, ITV is wondering where the 20-something audience has gone. And let's face it, the BBC hasn't fared a lot better in terms of retaining younger audiences. On top of failing to retain audiences, wider policy decisions will filter down to Children's, particularly if PSB is no longer a priority. For

example, the BBC is reducing BBC4 funding and winding down its commitment while Sky Arts are enjoying success. Similar things are happening in the Children's market. The system needs a rethink and reboot and that is what the PSM campaign is about.

The reality is that if we don't get the new PSM framework right for younger audiences, nothing else matters. The children's audience is the canary in the coal mine; you lose them, you lose the game. ⊙

5RIGHTS FOUNDATION AND THE UN CONVENTION ON THE RIGHTS OF THE CHILD

BARONESS BEEBAN KIDRON OBE

—

5Rights
FOUNDATION

It's official... Children's rights do apply in the digital world

The last year has been unlike any other. The impact of the pandemic has been seismic for us all, especially for children and young people. From remote education taking place over Microsoft Teams or Google Classroom, exam grades being decided by algorithms, zoom birthday parties, and stay at home orders, the world of the pandemic accelerated the impact of the digital world on childhood. All of which has made the formal recognition by the UN Committee on the Rights of the Child (CRC) that children's rights apply in the digital world that much more welcome.

United Nations

Convention on the Rights of the Child

The UN Convention on the Rights of the Child (UNCRC) is the most widely-ratified human rights treaty in history and provides a gold standard of how children's rights must be respected, protected and fulfilled by 196 signatory states. Since its adoption over 30 years ago the text has resolutely remained unchanged, but from time to time the Committee publish a General comment, that is an authoritative document that outlines how children's rights apply in a changing world.

General Comment No. 25 on children's rights in relation to the digital environment is one such document. After three years of consultation with hundreds of experts, 40 nation states

Lodovic Toinel, Unsplash

and UN bodies – and 69 workshops in 19 languages in 27 countries on 6 continents with 709 young people aged between 9 and 22 years old – it was adopted on 2nd March 2021.

The 5Rights General Comment Steering Group, acting on behalf of the Committee, brought together global perspectives on how children's rights should be applied to the digital world. Where the balance of participation and protection lay was fiercely debated. The needs of those with too much digital vs those who have yet to enjoy affordable access were put forward, and of course the joy of envisioning a digital world that anticipates and prepares for children's safe participation – all took our time and attention. Whatever the differences on the detail, there was an overwhelming consensus that digital environment must be designed and managed to embed children's rights at a systemic level and that states must ensure that businesses uphold their responsibilities to children. This consensus was mirrored by the views of children, who while being passionately keen to be part of the digital world are frustrated by its inequities and feel it should serve them and treat them better.

Below are just a selection of the many hundreds of views gathered:

"Generally it is a gigantic riddle what happens to our data, as it is hidden in complex data protection agreements and legal texts. I would like to obtain clarity about what really happens with my data."
Germany, girl, 16

"We would like the government, technology companies and teachers to help us manage untrustworthy information online."
Ghana, a group of children

"Websites and apps take and use our information, sometimes with our consent. But really, the fine print is so hidden that most people don't know what they've signed on to."
Canada, girl, 15

"Because we are exposed to several types of content and judged based on our social networking website profiles, we can end up losing our identity because of changes in how others see us."
Brazil, girl, 14:

"Just because I can use social media for free... [social media companies shouldn't be able to] use my data for free too. My personal data is still my privacy."
Philippines, girl, age unknown

Like the Convention itself, General Comment No 25 is universal: it applies for all signatory states, no matter the GDP of a country or the politics of the government. And for all children whatever their characteristics, abilities or circumstances. Crucially, it formally sets out for the first time that kids' rights apply online, explaining to states both why and how to act to make it a practical reality.

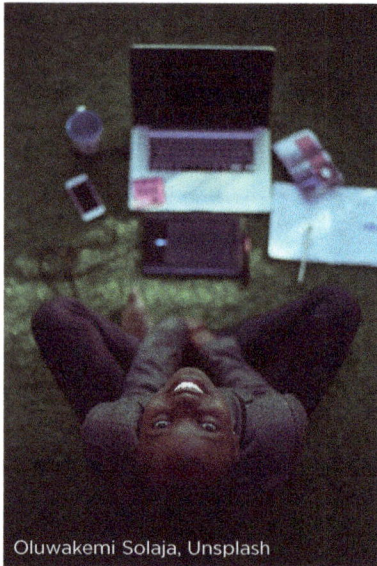

Oluwakemi Solaja, Unsplash

General Comment No 25 speaks to a digital environment that we are all in together. It calls for a greater emphasis on accessible technology and acknowledging the needs of children of varying abilities. It makes plain that discrimination is neither tolerated nor automated and explicitly mentions the many groups who are currently discriminated against to mandate their inclusion. Taking a systemic approach, it looks towards safety-by-design, privacy-by design, rights-by-design and is focused on the default settings that can enable children's participation in the digital world. For too long, responsibility has sat with the children and their parents, but General Comment No 25 changes this. In sum, General Comment No. 25 recasts the child as a rights holder in the digital world and puts responsibility on States and digital service providers to uphold children's rights.

The Committee has done what few authoritative bodies and governments have done and recognised that we have to apply our existing societal rules to the digital world. In doing so, it offers a bright light to the nearly one billion children who are online. At the exuberant and celebratory launch of the General Comment, Luis Pedernera, Chair of the UN Committee on the Rights of the Child, called on the global community to take General Comment No 25 and "make it yours and spread it to all corners of the world".

Children's Media Foundation readers, his call is to you. ⊙

CHILDREN'S RIGHTS IN THE DIGITAL SPACE

BY JOHN CARR

Following the development of the first web browsers the internet burst into the public's consciousness in the early to mid-1990s It came out of California with a "hippy vibe" and a halo. A great many household name businesses and Governments were caught unawares, typically by young entrepreneurs who had studied maths or computer sciences at elite Universities. Whether by accident or design, they quickly managed to position themselves and their fledgling companies somewhere in the vicinity of Albert Schweitzer, Ralph Nader and Mother Theresa, promising to make the world a better place, breaking the grip of lazy monopolies, undermining tyrants and bringing people together.

Caleb Williams, Unsplash

Who could argue with any of that? And in those early days everything on the internet was "free". In the minds of journalists, politicians and the wider public this helped cement the internet's counter cultural, benign disruptive image. It would be some time before we all realised that the image gained traction only because PayPal hadn't been invented and the distribution systems weren't yet in place because nobody had figured out what they could sell remotely as opposed to over a counter!

Harvesting personal data to facilitate targeted advertising was still some years away but would soon become the principal basis on which a substantial part of the entire virtual edifice would rest. The idea that the internet was "free" therefore persisted and provided a patina of philanthropy which was entirely undeserved. We might not be paying at the point of consumption, but we were paying in other ways, with our personal data. And "we" here included children even though that was likely unlawful because there can be no "fair processing" of the personal data of a child who does not understand the implications of saying "yes". Actually, in the early days we weren't even asked, at least not in a way that even Einstein could have understood.

Rohit Farmer, Unsplash

Macintosh Classic II
Jarrod Reed, Unsplash

facebook   1 Hacker Wa
Greg Bulla, Unsplash

Governments, anyone and everyone who asked about the soon evident downsides of the internet got the same answer from industry leaders. "Don't worry. We're cool. Look, we wear jeans, not suits. We know what we're doing with this incredibly complex stuff. We will do the right thing. Trust us." From these anarchic beginnings the idea of "self-regulation" took hold.

To help them on their way internet companies were even given unique legal protections, rendering them immune from legal liabilities which every other type of physical world business had to live by.

Not surprisingly, the first manifestation of this unprecedented protectionism came in the USA. It was prompted principally by the sudden explosion in the availability of graphic pornographic pictures, soon to be largely displaced by graphic pornographic videos in full colour with sound. It came in the form of the Communications Decency Act 1996 (CDA), perhaps the most inappropriately named legislative instrument in the history of legislative instruments. Far from attacking pornographers, as noted, it ended up giving them and a great many other types of online platforms unprecedented protections. Nevertheless, the measure was substantially and swiftly copied in the EU's e-Commerce Directive of 2000 and all the other liberal democracies outside the EU pretty much followed suit.

By removing the risk of legal liability, essentially online platforms were incentivised to do nothing to root out bad or illegal behaviour. In fact, if they tried to do anything they risked forfeiting their legal immunity. Some online businesses said their brand values were more important to them than retaining legal immunity so they told everyone they were taking steps to protect children from harmful content and behaviour but even here, because there was zero transparency or accountability, it was impossible for anyone to say if even the "the good guys" were doing as much as they could or should. Everything happened inside a black box. And for all those who publicly stated they were going to try to protect kids, many remained silent.

We all now know self-regulation has failed. Turns out the dudes didn't always know what they were doing with this "incredibly complex stuff". Sometimes they weren't "cool", breaking what little law there was time and again, often knowingly. But it took a long time for policymakers to gain enough understanding of the technology to feel sufficiently emboldened to confront the many challenges the laissez-faire regime had left unsolved. We are in the middle of that moment right now. I cannot think of a single major liberal democracy where "what to do about the internet" is not at or very near the top of the political agenda.

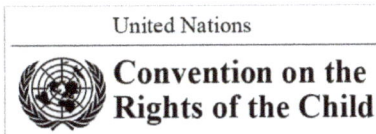

Elsewhere in this Yearbook there is an excellent account by some of the authors of the UNCRC General Comment. This is a reflection of the heightened level of global awareness to which I refer, in that instance specifically in relation to children. In the UK we have the "Online Safety Bill" (formerly the Online Harms Bill). In the EU, at the time of writing there are at least five major legislative measures in the works, each and all of which will impact on the position of children as internet users. A new European Centre is being developed to become a focal point for combatting online child sexual abuse and also to become a global Centre of Excellence to collect and disseminate best practice in terms of preventing child sexual abuse and providing support for victims. Last year the Audio-Visual Media Services Directive (AVMSD) took effect within the EU and because the UK was still in the EU at the time, the provision of the AVMD remain part of UK law. This imposes an obligation on the publishers of user generated video content which is likely to be harmful to children to ensure it is not "ordinarily" visible to children. That means age verification, but it has to be said the AVMSD has structural weaknesses which is why the Online Safety Bill will go further, at least for children in the UK.

Germany has introduced a radical new "Youth Protection Act". France has introduced a new law to restrict access to pornography sites by children. Australia, Canada and the USA are teeming with proposals. The list is long and while there definitely are variations between countries, what is striking are the similarities. Yet this is not surprising. It is true that cultural, economic and legal contexts can shift the emphasis one way or another, but the plain fact is children are the same everywhere and families everywhere have to face the same sorts of issues as their children start growing up and exploring the world around them as they get to know it and themselves better.

For all that those elements of Big Tech publicly now profess an acceptance of a need for regulation, the likes of Facebook and Google, to take two examples at random, are known to be mounting an unprecedented amount of lobbying in an attempt to "limit the damage" (as they see it). A key battleground will be the issue of liability. I have no problem with platforms retaining their immunity from criminal or civil actions but only if they can show they have made a reasonable attempt to anticipate risks to children arising from the way they provide their service, and have then taken all reasonable and proportionate steps to eliminate or mitigate those risks.

Companies should be under a legal obligation to have regard to available protective technologies and to deploy them to protect children, particularly against being exposed to illegal content and other forms of illegal activity.

Safety by design, privacy by default must become the watchwords. And above all there must be transparency. If a company says it does x, y or z to keep children safe someone, somewhere must be able to reassure children, parents, the public at large, Governments and law enforcement that it is not just a marketing slogan. Just as auditors certify a company's annual accounts represent a "true and fair view" of how the business has performed financially, we should have an independent agency which can certify that the claims made in an online business's terms and conditions are not just there for show. They mean something. Children deserve nothing less. ◯

YACF – TOGETHER

BY JACKIE EDWARDS

The DCMS-backed Young Audiences Content Fund is a community project; producers, broadcasters and the BFI team working together for young audiences. As a community we kept going for those audiences through the all of the everything that was 2020, even though it was sometimes hard to keep focussed on the future as events unfolded.

YACF development funding has proved itself through good times, but particularly through the challenging times of the last year. The Fund was a crucial support to many companies through lockdown, it kept some businesses going, but moreover kept creativity moving and the offer for young audiences growing and changing.

Many of the development projects we have supported have or are converting to broadcast commissions - definitely a good use of lockdown then! But ALL of the awarded projects kept people talking, connecting, employed, employing, all around the country. As you'd expect, with a few exceptions (e.g., shuffling writers' rooms on-line), development was less impacted than all of the planned dramas and factual entertainment on the production slate.

Production was a very different matter and projects were paused, reset, rescaled, ed specs rearranged to keep projects alive in spite of lockdown. That was very much a community project – but together, we did it.

A shared endeavour, to get through it and keep a clear eye on the future.

One of our favourite Fund catchphrases is 'Case by Case Basis', and that was true of helping keep various shows on the production road through the last year – no two shows had the same challenges or indeed solutions.

Some projects just kept going; animated projects like *Sali Mali* (Calon for S4C) and *Sol* (Paper Owl for S4C, TG4 and BBC ALBA) barely missed a beat and were delivered in time for Christmas. In fact, Sol turned into a dictionary definition of 'Together', when the indigenous language broadcasters came together for this beautiful Celtic co-pro. Commissioned pre-covid, the themes of loss and grief were all too pertinent for many of us last year. With this in mind, the producer, and commissioning broadcasters S4C, BBC ALBA and TG4, shared the programme with their English language PSB colleagues to reach the greatest audience, and it co-transmitted at Winter Solstice on CITV and ITV Hub, My5 and All4. It was another instance of the community holding hands together for the benefit of the audience.

Other shows re-tooled their ed spec to get through last year. Sky Kids current affairs show FYI had a reset which saw very smart use of Zoom, green screen, self-shoot at home, archive and very fancy graphics to deliver FYI Investigates, I Don't Get It and Kidversations pretty much on schedule and talking on hugely prescient topics and themes – nothing short of miraculous, and great for the audience.

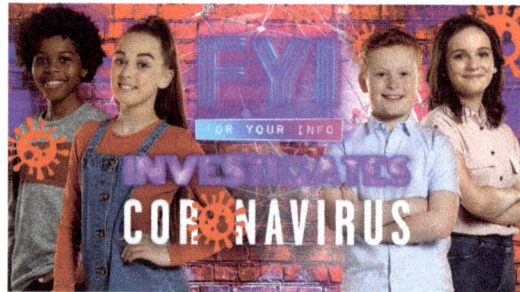

Some shows were designed for the situation such as *Letters in Lockdown* from Afro Mic, commissioned by E4 as a quick turnaround project – a beautiful, poignant mini-series which saw young people reaching out to loved ones they had been missing during lockdown by writing letters.

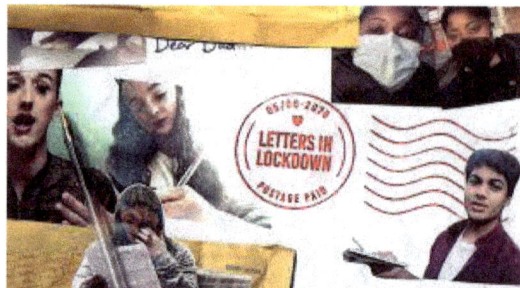

After the first lockdown, when they could, people dashed into studio last summer, and the likes of *How and Don't Unleash the Beast* were able to deliver and went out in the Autumn on CITV as planned.

Some shows had to accept that restrictions were simply too much of an impediment to their production and had to pause. Happily, all productions and partners stuck together and these shows are all set to resume or start production over the coming months.

Case by case it may be, but all have made progress despite conditions that have ranged from the difficult to the very, very, very difficult, through co-operation and conversation and just sticking together.

YACF funded shows that have landed are proving a point. Good content = good audiences = good business. Programmes aired quickly attracted audiences and consequently, re-commissions are coming thick and fast. These programmes are also receiving nominations and awards from telly beauty pageants as diverse as the content – Rose d'Or, Voice of the Listener and Viewer, RTS, Broadcast and the Rockies to name a few. Top reviews from audiences and peers are no bad thing. The fact that these shows got made at all is a testament to combined efforts of all.

Despite being apart, the industry stuck together to do the right thing by the audience. As well as the amazing programmes being developed and produced, we also set the audience a direct challenge during lockdown. See Yourself On Screen – SYOS - brought our community, broadcasters, producers, talent, trade bodies - all of us - together as we joined forces and put our arms around the audience to do something fun, challenging and distracting during the worst of times, which resulted in 15 made-at-home shows by young people broadcast on Milkshake!, E4, CITV, S4C and TG4 (we loved it so much we're doing it again this year – brace yourselves!) It was also an opportunity to talk to audiences and ask them how they were. In last year's SYOS challenge, 75% of the young participants said that they didn't see people that looked or sounded like them on television.

Which brings us to the point of the Fund really.

In the short two years that the Fund has been in existence, the development fund has supported 115 new projects that are currently converting to commissions at a rate of about 10% - double the industry standard and a sign of how a little resource can offer the structure and process to development that can really get results.

In the first two years the Fund has helped greenlight 45 brand new shows that have public service values at their heart. That's 187 hours greenlit for production and broadcast on Milkshake!, BBC ALBA, Channel 4, CITV, E4, ITVBe, TG4, Sky News, ITV2, KMTV and S4C, all of them programmes that reflect audiences from across the UK, that are inclusive in both creation and portrayal, have specific UK cultural relevance, will show us who we are, and will entertain, educate and inform.

If we can do so much together when we have to be apart, imagine what we can do together when our world is less constrained, and we can look toward a future that doesn't include the regular use of the words 'lateral', 'flow' or 'test'. In the now, when we're slowly being liberated, remember what can be done. We must go forward with optimism and keep making joyful content for our young. Public service television is our cultural glue – it shows us who we are and how to be. It brought us together when we were apart during lockdown and can help our way forward to a happier future, together.

EMIL AND THE DETECTIVES

Like everything in life, children's media is constantly changing, moving and evolving. Since March 2020, children's lives have changed, moved and evolved faster than we ever could have anticipated. In order to serve the audience in the best possible way, we must keep up with what's happening in their media lives with essential research. We reflect how the media world has changed in Covid.

LIFE IN LOCKDOWN
Bringing Families Together Through Content

MAXINE FOX

—

Giraffe Insights

After a year of lockdowns British kids have had it tough, changing restrictions have constantly shaken up kids viewing routines and home learning has blurred the worlds of entertainment and education. But now it seems like kids and families are finally finding their rhythm in the 'new normal'; going back to pre-pandemic routines and making permanent moves to viewing platforms that look to continue beyond lockdown. Within Giraffe Insights landmark study 'Kids and the Screen' we have seen children's viewing react to this tumultuous year of constant change and tracked these new routines as kids have settled into lockdown life.

Back to 'normal'?

The beginning of last year saw kids' viewing routines shift with kids viewing throughout the day flattening. Instead of peaking outside school hours in the morning and the later afternoon, viewing was also high in the middle of the day and early afternoon.

However, as lockdown continued into the winter of 2020, children reverted to pre-pandemic viewing patterns.

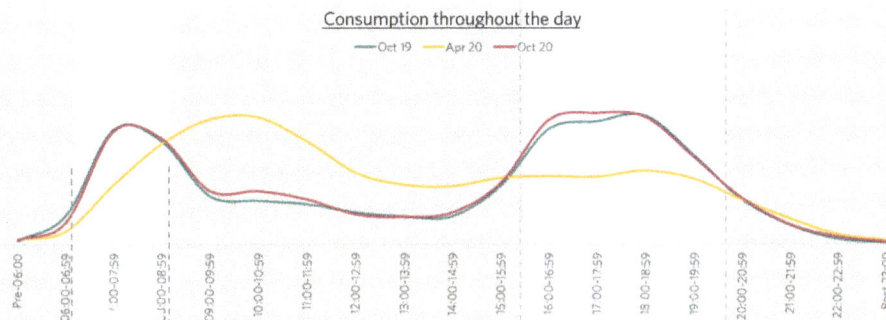

Consumption throughout the day

— Oct 19 — Apr 20 — Oct 20

Pre-06:00, 06:00-06:59, 07:00-07:59, 08:00-08:59, 09:00-09:59, 10:00-10:59, 11:00-11:59, 12:00-12:59, 13:00-13:59, 14:00-14:59, 15:00-15:59, 16:00-16:59, 17:00-17:59, 18:00-18:59, 19:00-19:59, 20:00-20:59, 21:00-21:59, 22:00-22:59, Post 23:00

Despite a slight mid-morning lift (around school break time) there isn't much change between kids viewing from late 2019 to late 2020. The initial shift in viewing routines appears to have been short lived as kids and adults adjusted to lockdown living. With virtual schooling and home working now the norm, families have settled back into regular viewing routines.

When it comes to how kids are watching content, there are also some behaviours that have returned to normal. Live TV viewing had been in steady decline for a while before 2020, however in early lockdown we experienced a levelling off of kids' live TV viewing with educational and family movie offerings driving this rise. However, during the final lockdown in the UK, viewing returned to normal with live TV continuing its decline, declining by 9% since 2018, alongside the continued rise of SVOD, increasing by 14% since 2018.

The connected TV is king

However, not everything is 'back to normal', a year of lockdowns has had a significant impact on what device kids are using to view. Kids are watching content on the 'main' TV significantly more than in recent years, with nearly 8 in 10 viewing occasions now occurring on the main living room TV screen. However, it's not live TV children are watching on the big TV, its SVOD. Nearly 50% of all the content watched on the main TV screen is on SVOD platforms, while only 39% of content is watched live. This shift is arguably caused by the rise of connected 'smart' TVs that allow access to SVOD, BVOD and digital content alongside live viewing.

Lockdown after lockdown has also meant kids are viewing less and less on the go. Viewing on devices such as tablets and mobile phones has declined significantly since 2019, with only 2 in 10 viewing occasions occurring on these portable devices.

The rise of connected smart TVs with built in access to SVOD platforms in combination with lockdown reducing kids' need for portable devices has meant that the main living room TV is now the key focal point for child and family viewing.

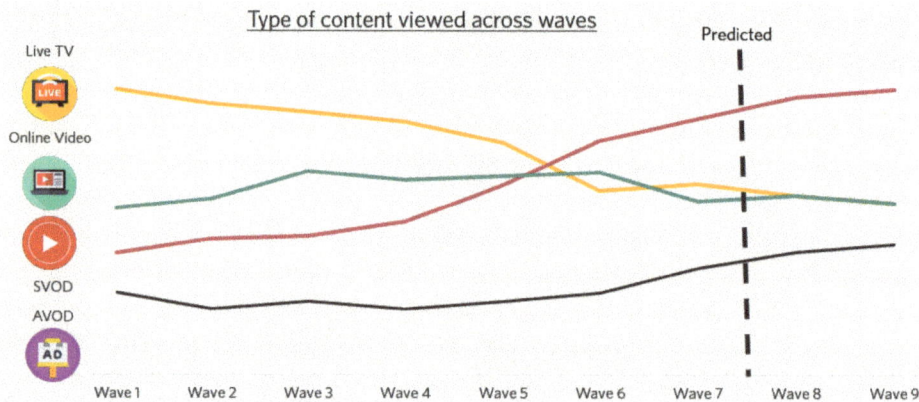

Type of content viewed across waves

Forget the SVOD wars, it's all about AVOD

We've all heard about the SVOD wars this year with Netflix, Amazon prime video and Disney + battling it out for total VOD supremacy. Although the SVOD battles are far from over, there is already a new challenger to the VOD crown.

In our tracking of kids' consumption, we have seen viewing through AVOD platforms significantly increase. Platforms such as Sky On Demand, All4 and the ITV Hub are increasingly taking up space in kids viewing schedules. Kids and families as a whole want to be able to view content at a time that suits them and access it all in one place. Whilst SVOD still remains a powerful tool, AVOD can offer kids and families their favourite TV content in one zone (e.g., Sky On Demand) and without charge (e.g., All4 and ITV Hub).

AVOD is also fast becoming a powerful tool for advertisers. AVOD platforms offer advertisers the opportunity to reach kids' audiences outside the more traditional routes of live broadcast, out of home and more recently online and through social media platforms.

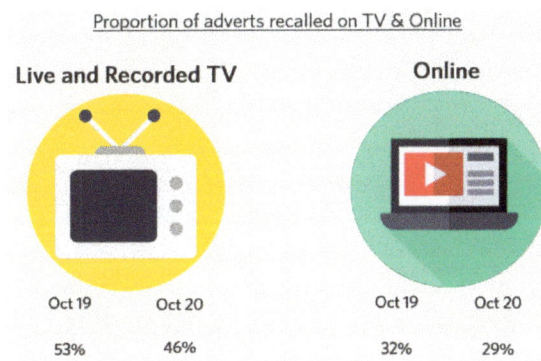

Proportion of adverts recalled on TV & Online

Live and Recorded TV — Oct 19: 53%, Oct 20: 46%

Online — Oct 19: 32%, Oct 20: 29%

Going forward, AVOD's rise throughout lockdown, alongside the decline in live TV viewing offers brands a new way of reaching engaged VOD audiences.

The slow decline of online

Since 2018, there has been a slow and steady decline in online viewing. However, arguably the biggest drop has been during lockdowns. This is interesting given the rise of other digital-first platforms such as SVOD & AVOD in the same period, despite the decline in viewing via portable devices.

Kids mostly view online content on their own, 59% of online viewing occasions are solo. However, throughout lockdown the majority of kids' viewing occasions have been shared either with siblings (34%) or parents (47%). This dominance of family viewing moments alongside the rise in the usage of the main TV screen over more individual devices such as mobile phones or tablets has certainly contributed to the decline in online.

This decline in online is mirrored by a small decline in YouTube viewing. Over the course of 2020 YouTube viewing dropped by 3%, with viewing of vloggers (once YouTube's bread and butter) falling by 10%. Instead of everyday, relatable vloggers, we see gamers and gaming content now topping the YouTube charts in their place. Gaming videos saw an increase in almost 10% during 2020 with top gaming youtubers such as **DanTDM**, **Ali A** and **Pewdiepie** drawing in crowds.

So, what does the future hold? Despite returning to some old habits, many things have changed for good. As children have become used to the turbulence of lockdown life, they have formed new habits around SVOD and more recently AVOD content, with the smart TV now the anchor of kids viewing worlds. As we move into a post-lockdown era, we will likely see a rise in portable device usage as kids travel more outside of the home. Despite this, we predict online may well still struggle overall to compete with the dominance of SVOD & AVOD platforms, however the personability and breadth of content it hosts will likely maintain its position in kids' media ecosystems. AVOD platforms will certainly be a key media asset for brands and advertisers wanting to reach both kids and families, with content that brings the family together undoubtedly the biggest winner to come out of a life in lockdown. ○

CONTROL OVER CHOICE:
What Children Have Chosen To Consume During The COVID-19 Pandemic

HELEN LOCKETT AND AFRA ACQUAH

In March 2020, COVID 19 hit and the UK along with the rest of the world went into a lockdown akin to a Hollywood disaster movie. It's fair to say that young people's lives have been hugely disrupted – school happening at home, parents/guardians doubling up as teachers, and children being separated from friends and family members outside their immediate households. Despite the loss of routine and a lack of certainty about when and if life will return to how it was before, there is one aspect that has remained a constant: the presence of media and technology in children's lives.

Discovery's kids and youth division – The Hub – has been carrying out a qualitative tracker with young audiences for almost 10 years looking at how kids' and teens' behaviours, attitudes and perceptions change over time. A key focus of discussion is their media consumption and what their media world looks like. Our latest wave was carried out in November 2020, where we spoke to 34 young people aged between 7-22yrs from a diverse range of backgrounds, remotely over Zoom. We utilised a mix of approaches, from one-on-one depth interviews, friendship pairs, triads and mini-groups, as well as capturing pre and post vox pop videos to bring our insights to life.

Over the last few years, we have seen the children's media landscape shift and evolve drastically, impacting how, when, where and what children and teens are consuming. We've witnessed:

- The age of first personal device getting ever younger

- Traditional broadcast TV viewing declining steadily, and at the same time, use of (S) VOD services and on demand content rapidly increasing

- A growth in bingeing culture and watching all of something at once, right now

- Increased interest in creating media content not just consuming it!

An overarching thread emerging from each research dip we conduct is the need for children and teens to have **control over choice**. Control over choice means the ability to choose what they want to consume, when they want to consume it and with zero effort! Following a year in which young people have been feeling quite out of control, having control over the media they consume has been more important than ever.

So, how is control over choice playing out during a pandemic? We've found five key trends:

1. Technology has been a lifeline

Piotr Cichosz, Unsplash

2020 marked the start of a period where technology replaced 'real life'! It has been an essential way for children to stay in touch with their friends and family and can be a respite when they are confined indoors. Some children reported being given more freedom to spend greater amounts of time on their devices than they had before the pandemic begun, as their parents seek to lessen the blow of their lives changing so drastically by giving them access to the enjoyable aspects of life that are still possible.

2. Social media and gaming are key places for conversation and distraction

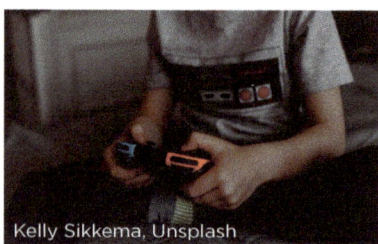
Kelly Sikkema, Unsplash

While children had already been communicating virtually before the pandemic, not being able to see each other in person means it has been taking on an even greater role in children's day-to-day lives. What we found interesting is how media platforms have become a place for kids to hang out with friends as well as consume content. While Snapchat and Instagram remain popular amongst teenagers (but no mentions of WhatsApp), emerging platforms like TikTok are used not just for their media content but also for communicating. 'What's your number?' has been replaced with 'What's your Snapchat or TikTok?', with phone numbers seen as a functional way to gain access to content platforms.

Amongst boys particularly, gaming has become a regular way to spend time with their friends, especially if they do not have social media accounts of their own yet. The party and chat function on consoles like the Xbox has been allowing groups of friends to talk out loud to one another whilst gaming, adding to the fun and making them feel less 'cut off' from their social circle. This means it has become even more important to have the same consoles and games as their friends – not just for social cache, but for being able to be social full stop.

3. Households are using a wider variety of content providers

Clement M Jiop, Unsplash

From an entertainment perspective, YouTube is still one of the most consistently used (S)VODs for children of all ages. It exemplifies control over choice in its ability to bring a wide range of relevant content to them via an engaging interface that makes finding and choosing content simple for even the youngest children.

With linear TV viewing offering less control over choice, linear time has been minimal compared to time spent on (S)VODs and social platforms. Instead, households have been signing up to different (S)VOD platforms giving children a wider array of choice – Disney+ is a common new addition. However, Netflix is still the most popular platform overall, with its visually appealing design, easy to use interface and personalised / tailored content - all cited as plusses.

4) Lockdown has increased demand for funny and light hearted content, and diverse content

Emily Wade, Unsplash

Children have been watching a range of content on (S) VOD platforms, from *The InBESTigators*, *The Fresh Prince of Bel Air* and *Brooklyn Nine-Nine* on Netflix, *His Dark Materials* on iPlayer, *Lucifer* on Prime Video and *The Descendants* and *Avengers* on Disney+. However, a theme evident in the types of content they're watching is that to counter the uncertainty and heaviness of the pandemic, they're looking for light-hearted content to distract themselves.

Singing and general 'day in the life' videos by The Labrant Family, music playlists / videos, funny challenges from **The Sidemen**, fitness videos from **Chloe Ting** and watching people play games such as *Minecraft*, are just a few examples of content children have been consuming on YouTube. TikTok has been a popular source of entertainment, with children whiling away hours watching dance challenges and funny skits shared by young social media stars during lockdown.

A few older children also said they felt there had been increase in more diverse films and series on (S)VOD services, and the Black American teen sitcom *Sister Sister* is one such example. In our research, we have found diversity is important to younger generations, and can affect the types of media children want to consume as much as the organisations they want to support.

5) Content is also playing a role in education and creativity

Patricia Prudente, Unsplash

When it comes to 'educating', some children said they have watched more news than usual. This has tended to be live on linear TV, instigated by parents, and often about COVID 19. BBC iPlayer has played an educational role with younger children specifically, whose parents have used the Bitesize content to support their learning. We all know the popularity of **Joe Wicks'** PE lessons during lockdown, but YouTube is still children's Google in a broader sense and a trusted place to go to watch videos to support their homework and studies too. TikTok and YouTube have also encouraged creativity amongst children who have been filming their own TikToks and taking part in viral challenges, filming vlogs and editing them, and getting ideas on crafting activities or make-up techniques.

Overall, we've found that previous trends of increased media consumption and control over choice have been amplified during lockdown, since children have had fewer options for how to spend their free time. What remains to be seen is the impact post-pandemic.

Will households continue to subscribe to multiple (S)VOD services, and will demand for diverse and humorous content continue to increase? Watch this space – we certainly will.

ROBLOX IN LOCKDOWN

NIKKI STEARMAN

Covid-19 restrictions have limited children's opportunities to play in real-world spaces over the last year. Have the lockdowns increased opportunities for digital play? For 7–12-year-olds, it has all been happening on Roblox...

As a game designer at Dubit, I assumed that during this last year UK children have been spending more time playing games on devices. After all, we've all increased our screen time over 2020, right? Well, no, actually.

Dubit trend data compared the amount of time spent gaming on devices from April 2019 to October 2020 for children aged 7 - 12 in the UK. The average time per week spent gaming was a consistent 2 - 3 hours a week. It hadn't changed significantly at all. What has changed over lockdown is what games they like to play.

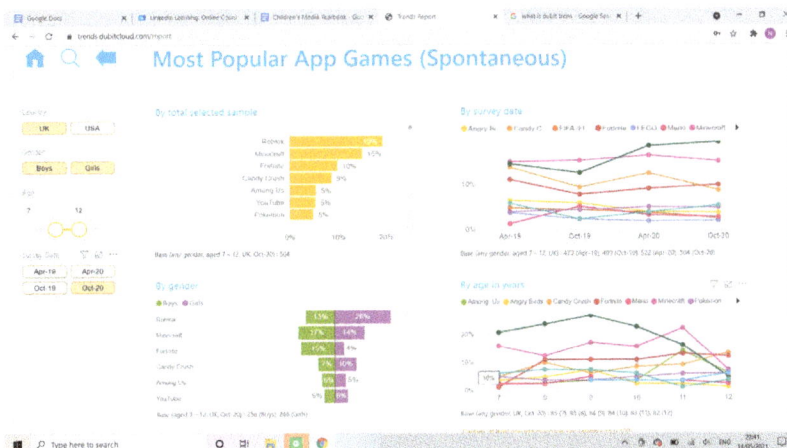

Preferred games (open-ended question) of 7-12 years old in the UK

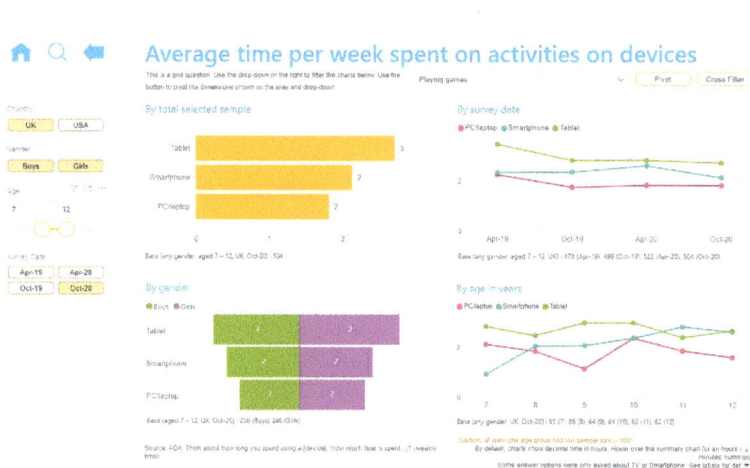

Device usage of 7-12 years old in the UK in the last week (October 2020)

Roblox is at the top of the list of 'games they would like to play' for this age group with 13% of boys and 26% of girls rating it as one of their most preferred games, beating *Minecraft* and *Fortnite* as a must have choice overall in October 2020.

It was played by 45% of 7–12-year-olds in the last week. *Roblox* is on the up.

For those of you unfamiliar with *Roblox* - it is a platform for games created with Roblox Studio, which is free to use. As a result, user generated content makes up the vast majority of games. It's like YouTube for gaming!

Roblox continues to grow - it currently has over 165 million monthly active users and huge reach - 24 games have over **1 billion plays** and **10,000 games have over 1 million plays on its platform**.

So why do 7–12-year-olds like Roblox so much? Here are my top 5 reasons.

1. There are SO MANY games to play on this platform.

If you don't like a game, you can find another one to replace it very quickly. If you do like a game, you can follow it and favourite it to find it again - like subscribing to a YouTube channel. Games are categorized by most popular so can quickly gather momentum as the best rises to the top. Games are sorted by genre so you'll find something you enjoy, and with the content changing and updating regularly, there is a constant reason to return.

2. You'll always have friends!

Roblox is a multiplayer experience - you play with others. The best *Roblox* games are the ones that design for how children play together. For example, in a Story game players can give each other hints to solve problems via the Chat function. In a dance game, you may be relying on other players to rate your performance. You don't have to be alone.

Cruise Story in Roblox

44

3. It uses real play patterns but in fantastical, magical settings!

Roblox uses play styles and game types that are familiar to children. Love obstacle courses? Great! Play an "obby" but in the Tower of Doom instead. Play Hide and Seek - but not in your regular garden, why not a huge forest? And what if you could change into different things or turn invisible altogether? Your imagination is the only limit.

Go Noodle Hide and Seek

4. Your avatar stays with you in every game you play

Children love creating an online avatar to represent themselves in digital play. What is really clever about Roblox, is that identity stays with them on the platform regardless of the game they play. It means avatar personalization is big business on Roblox and players can invest heavily in looking their best as a symbol of their status.

5. You can make your own content

Roblox is mostly user generated content. Anyone can make a game on the platform using Roblox Studio which means as fans of the platform have grown older, the community of creators has too. It's the starting point for many kids learning to code.

Ian Douthwaite, CEO at Dubit says: "Kids are learning to code in there but this is constantly overlooked. We talk about creating more coders - often in education-led initiatives that scream "school", but in Roblox these kids are entrepreneurial coders already!"

In the US, the top Roblox games make **$50 million (£35.3 million)** a year!

What does this mean for the future? As we leave lockdown and the restrictions are behind us, I believe that Roblox will continue to grow for this audience. Hopefully those gaming hours remain consistent and Roblox is where children choose to spend them.

CHILDREN'S MEDIA USE IN LOCKDOWN

CAROLINE CASSON

—

Ofcom

2020 was an extraordinary year, and one that had a profound impact on children's media use. For children in particular, education, socialisation and other formative experiences were disrupted or suspended. This led to children having a huge increase in free time and ultimately, changes and developments in their media behaviours.

This article draws largely on Ofcom's annual quantitative Children and Parents' Media Use and Attitudes Tracker, which provides detailed evidence on media access, use, and understanding among children aged 3-15 (and their parents). And our Children's Media Lives research, a qualitative research project, designed as a way of providing a small-scale, rich and detailed qualitative complement to our quantitative survey.

RESEARCH TIMELINE

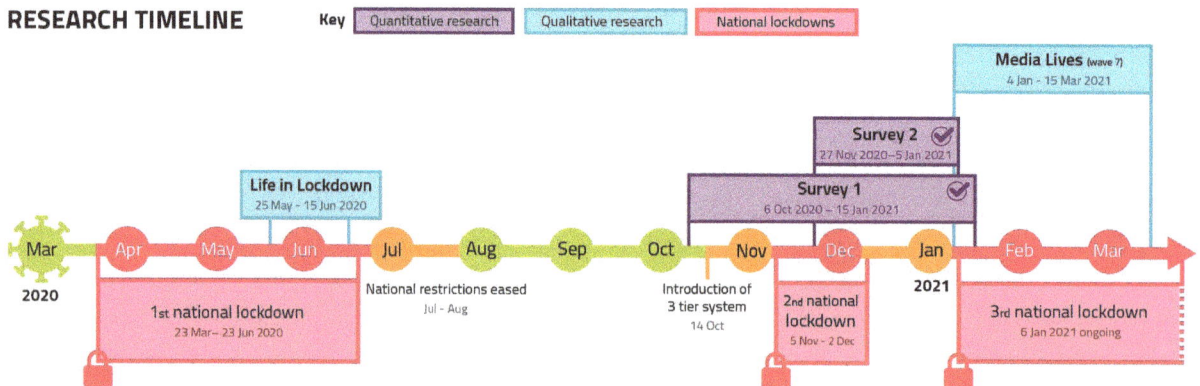

Key: Quantitative research · Qualitative research · National lockdowns

Media Lives (wave 7)
4 Jan - 15 Mar 2021

Survey 2
27 Nov 2020 – 5 Jan 2021

Survey 1
6 Oct 2020 – 15 Jan 2021

Life in Lockdown
25 May - 15 Jun 2020

Mar 2020 | Apr | May | Jun | Jul | Aug | Sep | Oct | Nov | Dec | Jan 2021 | Feb | Mar

1st national lockdown
23 Mar– 23 Jun 2020

National restrictions eased
Jul - Aug

Introduction of 3 tier system
14 Oct

2nd national lockdown
5 Nov - 2 Dec

3rd national lockdown
6 Jan 2021 ongoing

Children's use of video-sharing platforms (VSPs) was almost universal.

Children were engaging in a wide range of activities to keep them entertained during 2020. In particular, use of video-sharing platforms, or VSPs, was almost universal among children: 97% of 5-15s engaging in this activity. Covid-19 increased this behaviour; seven in ten children aged 8-15 said they had used VSPs more during 2020 than before.

YouTube was the most-used VSP among children aged 5-15 for watching content in 2020 (87%); followed by 47% watching TikTok, Instagram (37%), Facebook (34%), or Snapchat (33%). A minority used Go Noodle (6%), Vimeo (6%), Dailymotion (4%) and Dubsmash (4%).

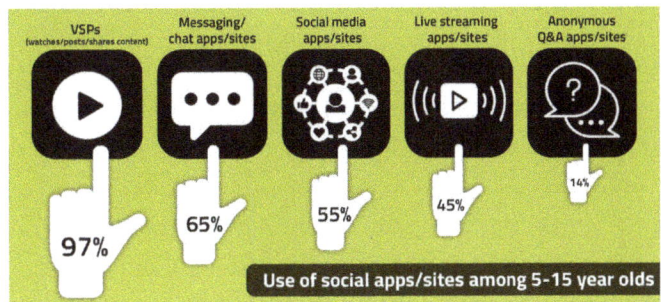

Consuming content on VSPs was more popular than posting or sharing

While a majority of children were watching content on VSPs, over half said they posted or shared content : ranging from 39% of 5-7s to 75% of 12-15s.

No single platform was used by a majority of children for posting or sharing content; around a quarter used TikTok (26%), YouTube (23%), Instagram (22%), Snapchat (22%) or Facebook (20%).

Children watched a variety of content on VSPs and tended to seek content they could 'relate' to

Among all 5-15s, the majority nominated funny videos, jokes, pranks, and challenges to watch on VSPs (80%).

Meanwhile, almost half said they watched vloggers or YouTube influencers. Some of our Children's Media Lives participants said they followed influencers to whom they felt they could relate to, even if

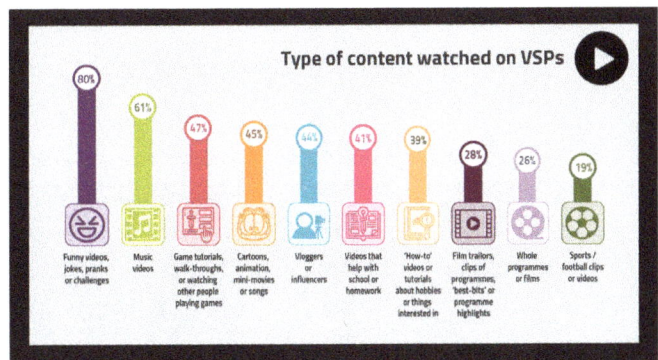

their lifestyles or appearance differed from their own. For example, one participant said that British YouTubers that she followed were more similar to her than some of the more famous YouTubers. While another participant, who followed body-sculpting and weightlifting influencers, said that he found them aspirational and relatable.

The majority of older children were aware of vloggers being sponsored by brands

Two-thirds of children aged 12-15 correctly recognised that vloggers or influencers might be being paid by companies or brands to promote their products or services (65%). While a third thought the vloggers either just wanted to share the information with their followers, or that they thought the product or service was cool or good to use.

The participants in our Children's Media Lives study understood that influencers were paid to promote content. But rather than annoying them, some reported finding this helpful as it showed them things that were in line with their interests.

Up to a fifth of 8-15 year-olds have 'gone live' via streams

In 2020, almost half of children aged 8-15 said they had used live streaming services to watch other people's live streams and live videos; Older children, aged 12-15, were more likely to say they had 'gone live' themselves, by sharing their own videos with others (17% vs. 8% of 8-11s).

Among the older age group, Instagram Live and YouTube Live were the sites or apps most likely to be used (38% and 32% respectively among 12-15s), followed by a quarter using Facebook Live. While YouTube Live was also the most likely to be used by 8-11-year-olds (by 30%), around one in ten used Instagram Live or Facebook Live. Meanwhile, Twitch, one of the leading streaming platforms for gamers, was used by 7% of 5-15s overall.

The Covid-19 pandemic hastened the trend towards alternative devices for watching TV programmes

Watching TV programmes was also a key form of entertainment during 2020, among 98% of 5-15s. However, how children watch TV is changing. For the first time, children were as likely to watch TV content on an alternative device (83%), as on

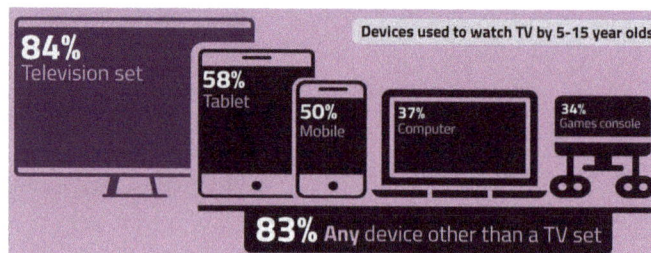

Devices used to watch TV by 5-15 year olds

84% Television set
58% Tablet
50% Mobile
37% Computer
34% Games console

83% Any device other than a TV set

a TV set (84%).

Of the alternative devices used, 58% used a tablet, while 50% watched on a mobile phone. More than a third watched on a laptop or desktop, or on a games console or player.

Video-on-demand overtook live TV as children's choice for content

The pandemic also appears to have accelerated the trend towards video-on-demand (VoD) content over live TV. In 2020, almost all 5-15s watched any type of VoD content (96%) compared to 56% watching live broadcast TV.

While use of all VoD services increased in 2020, use of subscription-video-on-demand services (SVoD) was by far the most popular.

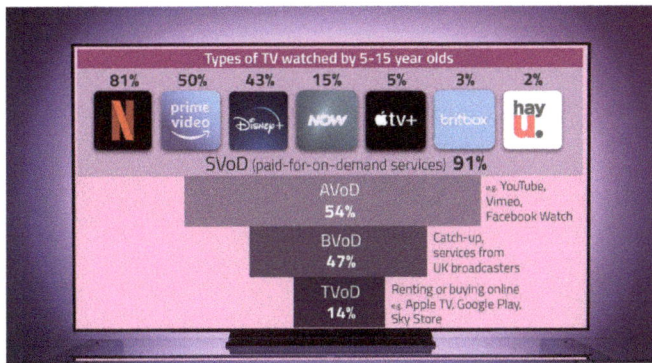

Types of TV watched by 5-15 year olds

| 81% | 50% | 43% | 15% | 5% | 3% | 2% |

SVoD (paid-for-on-demand services) 91%

AVoD 54% — e.g. YouTube, Vimeo, Facebook Watch

BVoD 47% — Catch-up, services from UK broadcasters

TVoD 14% — Renting or buying online e.g. Apple TV, Google Play, Sky Store

As in previous waves of our Children's Media Lives study, none of the children in our sample were watching live television regularly. In fact, while they might use the term 'watching TV' occasionally, they predominantly used it to refer to watching on-demand content.

Figures from BARB (the UK TV audience measurement body) also show the overall decline in watching broadcast TV content among children. In 2020, children aged 4-15 watched an average of 6 hours 54 minutes of broadcast content on the TV set per week – down by 35 minutes since 2019.

Substantial minorities of children did not feel well enough represented within TV programmes and films

As with the proportions of children watching vloggers that they felt they can relate to, the same could be said for those watching TV programmes and films (whether on broadcast TV or on-demand). In 2020, a substantial minority of children aged 8-15 felt there were not enough programmes that

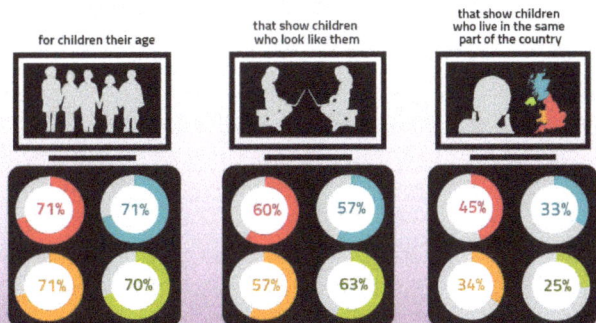

Differing views by UK nation of representation in programmes

Proportion of 8-15 year olds in England, Scotland, Wales, and N Ireland who believe there are enough TV programmes...

for children their age — 71% 71% / 71% 70%

that show children who look like them — 60% 57% / 57% 63%

that show children who live in the same part of the country — 45% 33% / 34% 25%

included children from the same part of the country as them (35%), that showed children that looked like them (23%) or were for children their age (22%). The below graphic shows the proportions of children who felt there were enough programmes reflecting this, across the UK nations.

Further information

To find out more about our Making Sense of Media programme and for details on how to join our network, please go to https://www.ofcom.org.uk/making-sense-of-media

For more information on MSOM, and Ofcom's other media literacy research, please visit: https://www.ofcom.org.uk/research-and-data/media-literacy-research/publications. ○

THE SECRET GARDEN

Do we ever know what's going on in the minds of others? Children's mental health has taken a real battering in lockdown and it's important to recognise the effect the past year has had on young lives. It's not all doom and gloom, however, and children have shown a remarkable ingenuity and resilience in finding ways of being together, even when they're not..

Adrian Holmes, Unsplash

CHILDREN'S MENTAL HEALTH

SALLYANN KEIZER

—

"There comes a point where we need to stop just pulling people out of the river. We need to go upstream and find out why they're falling in."
Desmond Tutu

What role do we as children's content makers, consultants and educators play in the rapidly changing landscape of children's mental health?

Children's mental health is a passion of mine and has been since I studied child development many moons ago. So, when I first met **Professor Elaine Fox** from Oxford University in 2012, and she shared her work in the area of neuroscience, emphasising the power we all have in nurturing our own mental wellbeing, building up our emotional resilience, and learning how to navigate those ups and downs of life with greater ease, I was hooked. As a journalist and children's content maker I embarked upon a personal and professional journey to explore how we empower our younger generation to flourish.

Mental Health UK

Almost a decade later, this work has become more important than ever. Over the years, increasing awareness of the importance of mental health has led to research revealing the key facts and figures of the wellbeing of our younger generation. Latest data from www.mentalhealth.org.uk suggests that half of children's mental health problems are established by age 14, and 75% by 24 years old. Furthermore, the stats show that in any given year a fifth of adolescents may experience a mental health problem.

It is still a matter of debate in the world of mental health research whether the apparent rise in mental illness is largely a result of better recognition and reporting or, more concerningly, an actual increase in prevalence. However, when research shows us that ¾ of young people that meet clinical criteria for anxiety and depression go unrecognised and unrecorded in intervention statistics, it's clear that we are facing a crisis on some level, and one that has potential to escalate following the events of the past year. Young people who already have recognised mental health needs have reported a worsening of their condition, and children as young as four are experiencing increased feelings of loneliness and anxiety.

These facts in many ways paint a bleak picture, and the challenges are indeed vast. However, my journey has taken me across many realms within the world of mental health, and has given me reason to think that the state of affairs is more hopeful than it may at first seem. For much of history, mental health research has focused on the 'negative' aspects of the human condition – mental illnesses, struggles and suffering. In recent years, though, there has been a big shift as academics have begun to research the science of human wellness, happiness and flourishing. As a result, we now know how things like kindness, self-compassion, mindfulness and gratitude impact us on an emotional and neurological level. For children, these effects may be amplified: the child's brain is the most wonderfully malleable (or 'plastic') thing, and the habits that are laid down from the very beginning of a child's life will go on to shape the remainder of their years. The high stakes that this fact entails have already been seen through the figures I shared above. Yet, instead of focusing on what we have 'lost' or what problems our society has accumulated, should we not ask ourselves what we can gain, and how we can work in tandem with the remarkable minds of our children to carve better futures together?

This is where I believe the media can come in. For better or for worse, screen time is on the rise - 45% of parents reported this as a concern during lockdown. Besides their family and their friends, the characters and work we create in the world of Children's are the most constant companions of the kids of today. This is why I feel that media is where mental health education belongs, and why I decided to take action. So, as lockdown hit in March

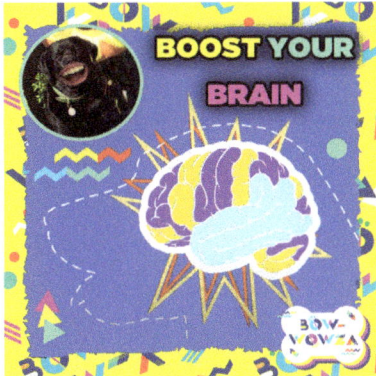

Joe Sniffs

Kayley

2020 and our CBeebies series ground to a halt, I shifted the whole of my team across to my passion project of five years, our non-profit www.bow-wowza.com. It's a world of talking dogs and wellbeing hacks equipping children to be mentally resilient, full of 'pawsitivity' and preparing them to unleash their best lives.

Just as we encourage regular exercise and brushing our teeth daily, we can nurture positive habits from an early age when it comes to children's emotional wellbeing. Alongside the canine comedy came the culmination of years of work with child psychologists and psychiatrists, academics, educators and consultants, all interwoven into our content and narratives. Videos, meditations, and creative activities to inspire children everywhere were produced and a year later we have just launched our 8-module schools' package, which is reaching thousands of children around the UK. While we are pursuing a broadcast route, the offering as it stands is 100% free of charge. The sole vision is to empower children to flourish.

Some may question the logic of this decision, and query whether it is the way to create 'real' change. But what is real change? What is the balance between reaching millions of children through a mainstream series or brand and delivering transformation through encouraging fewer to take up regular mentally healthy habits? This is something that has always fascinated me - the tension between reach and impact, breadth and depth. While the goal is to achieve both, I feel just as confident with a smaller offering in schools which truly embeds the work into children's young minds and beings as I would with a million-dollar commission, or more. This is because I believe change comes through actions, not slogans - creating a culture of emotional resilience is a practical task. Wellbeing is a learnable skill like any other and a cultural value that can be embedded into our work.

So, just as we have been urged for years to take a step back and ask ourselves, 'Why is that main character

not a girl?'; 'How can we improve the inclusion in our content?', similarly I think we can ask: what mental health messages, subtle or otherwise are we sharing with our children? And just as we look at the Diversity and Inclusion off-screen, how can we address the mental wellbeing culture of our organisations and companies too? The messages that children absorb are not confined to the straight lines of their screens, and I firmly believe that the value of any advocacy my work expresses is diminished if the culture of my company and the wellbeing of my staff do not match up. So the question I want to leave you with is this: what small changes can you make, socially, professionally or even personally, that will add to the world's pot of happiness?

We do all have control over our own happiness, and as media makers we have the special responsibility of exerting influence over other people's, too. So, let's appreciate this power as the gift that it is, and take equally good care of our viewers, our colleagues and ourselves. ⬭

PLAYING TO STAY CONNECTED

SONIA LIVINGSTONE AND KRUAKAE POTHONG

A surge in demand for online communication services during the Covid-19 lockdown is hardly surprising. Yet the range of inventive uses of digital technologies to stay connected with dispersed friends and families may stretch digital providers' imaginations!

Neonbrand-Rhoz, Unsplash

5Rights
FOUNDATION

The Digital Futures Commission was established by the 5Rights Foundation to identify what **good** looks like for children in a digital world, and to embed children's best interests in the design of their digital futures. Having quickly learned how rarely children's views are sought, yet how vocal children can be regarding their rights in relation to the digital environment,[1] we held a public consultation on play during the winter of 2020-2021.[2]

Since COVID-19 meant people's lives suddenly became digital-by-default,[3] we learned about a host of tactics invented by the 126 participants, half of them children and young people, half of them parents, carers or professionals working with young people, who joined our 28 lively online group discussions. This was a fortuitous time for our research, as the public, including children and young people, has had ample cause to reflect on the importance of digital technologies in their lives, including the challenges it brings.[4]

They have also had ample cause to invent new ways to survive these peculiar times, including creatively adapting digital technologies to serve their playful purposes. A mother and theatre practitioner told us:

"My eight-year-old was playing on Zoom... The kids... all have access to the screen, and they're sort of playing hide and seek or catch [or] tag, so someone has to draw; someone has to be the eraser."

A fourteen-year-old girl baked cake with her sister over WhatsApp to *"connect"* while living apart during lockdown. A family told us how they play quizzes as part of their *"big zoom"* session to *"catch up"* with relatives. A mother and daughter described playing *"Scattergories"* with their dispersed family via Zoom. An eighteen-year-old young woman combined Discord with Google Forms to create an *"element of quizzes and trivia"* when having fun with her friends. A pastoral school worker has been running various activities, including *"Play-Doh"*, *"treasure hunt games"* and *"cooking"* online as part of the after-school club.

In addition to integrating what originated as physical and tactile play into the digital environment, participants also brought play from the digital domain into their physical world. A sixteen-year-old girl from Cardiff reported mimicking the game mechanics of the online multiplayer social deduction game *Among Us* with her classmates in school. A Year 6 teacher wryly observed the transfer of digitally-originated fun to the physical playground in school:

"I think TikTok is the new skipping. All we ever see are children walking around doing these movements, and they all know the same movements."

As young as nine years old, our young participants also reported adapting forms of online communication to coordinate their play on screens with their peers when playing games such as *Minecraft*, *Roblox* and *Call of Duty*. They adapted various communication tools and platforms, ranging from a simple phone to social media (e.g., House Party) and digital communication platforms, such as Discord, WhatsApp and Zoom, to support voice communication during gameplay. As a father of a nine-year-old girl observed:

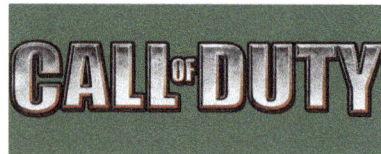

"They build houses and interact with each other in whatever world they've generated. But then they're also always doing it with a Houseparty, Zoom call type thing ... they can all talk to each other and play a bit. They're using it as a means of social interaction at the moment."

Irrespective of how families improvise using digital technologies for fun, two common qualities of play shine through – intrinsically motivated and socially connected.[5] Playing to stay connected, especially during lockdown, means improvising digital communication platforms, such as Zoom and Google Forms that were designed for business use. But it turns out they can also enable traditional, physical and tactile play online if the players are sufficiently intrinsically motivated. Lockdown play links friends and family together through common tasks, such as quizzes, world-building projects, or coordinating actions in digital games, and this in turn generates further conversations about their shared experience.

Seeking to stay connected through play during lockdown has diversified the forms of hybrid play well beyond the original design objectives of available digital technologies, including games. Such hybrid play does not require advanced technology such as the augmented reality of *Pokémon Go*. Participants in our consultation found their own ways to bring traditional, physical play like hide-and-seek or treasure hunts online. Through their imaginations, they opened up unforeseen opportunities for integrating physical, tactile playful activities into digital fun, and vice versa. In the process, they found a solution to the thorny problem of "screen time."[6]

What conditions, then, are needed to cultivate these hybrid opportunities? The way our participants improvised digital technologies to satisfy the intrinsically motivated and social qualities of their play highlights three enabling features: communication, adaptability and hybridity. Digital communication features enable people to socialise during and after their play experience, especially when physical contact is limited. Adaptability refers to the design of digital products and services that make them more malleable for flexible use without changing their core functions. Hybridity connects playful experiences across multiple spaces and contexts of use.

So, how can we improve play in the digital environment? The range of digital communication tools and platforms used by our participants in their play suggests a healthy level of diversity in terms of communication channels and practices. However, participants called for more effective implementation of safeguarding measures, such as content, contact and conduct moderation and filters on the digital communication channels they use, and guidance on safety measures. They called for more flexible and adaptable design to enable them to negotiate their own interaction opportunities. These calls for change indicate that digital providers should prioritise safe, ethical and open-ended design, and leave the rest to people's imagination and capacity to improve.

Endnotes

[1] Mukherjee, S. and Livingstone, S. (2020) Children and Young People's Voices. Digital Futures Commission. London: 5Rights Foundation. Available at https://digitalfuturescommission.org.uk/wp-content/uploads/2020/10/Children-and-Young-Peoples-Voices.pdf

[2] Livingstone, S. (2020) A consultation on play in a digital world launches the Digital Futures Commission. Digital Futures Commission blog, available at https://digitalfuturescommission.org.uk/blog/a-consultation-on-play-in-a-digital-world-launches-the-digital-futures-commission/

[3] Livingstone, S. (2020) Digital by default: the new normal of family life under COVID-19. LSE British Politics and Policy blog, available at https://blogs.lse.ac.uk/politicsandpolicy/digital-by-default/

[4] Pothong, K. (2021) Reimagining digital play: we want more sociability, hybridity and safety, with fewer tricky freemiums. Digital Futures Commission blog, available at https://digitalfuturescommission.org.uk/blog/reimagining-digital-play-we-want-more-sociability-hybridity-and-safety-with-fewer-tricky-freemiums/

[5] Cowan, K. (2020). A Panorama of Play – A Literature Review. Digital Futures Commission. London: 5Rights Foundation. Available at https://digitalfuturescommission.org.uk/wp-content/uploads/2020/10/A-Panorama-of-Play-A-Literature-Review.pdf

[6] Livingstone, S. and Blum-Ross, A. (2020) Interview about Parenting for a Digital Future. LSE Review of Books. Available at https://blogs.lse.ac.uk/lsereviewofbooks/2020/08/07/author-interview-q-and-a-with-sonia-livingstone-and-alicia-blum-ross-authors-of-parenting-for-a-digital-future/

LET THE CHILDREN PLAY TOGETHER - EVEN IF IT IS VIRTUAL

BY GARY POPE

—

KidsIndustries
the family agency™

I could tell you that the explosion of gaming in the hearts, minds and wallets of our children is because of technical advancement, because of wonderful narrative and compelling characters, because of the nefarious arts of marketing, or because of the addictive nature of the soon to be banned loot crates.

But I won't, because it is far, far more fundamental (and simple) than that.

Let's start with a little story...

Laurence changed schools in Year 4. He had a real hard time from some of the other kids. New boy and all that. He wasn't really bothered - which was a relief. But it wasn't a great way to spend the first summer term in a new school.

Then Fortnite happened.

Turned out he wasn't bad at it. In fact, he was pretty good. You see, at heart it's a social thing and Laurence always played nicely with the other kids. And pretty soon, having proven himself expert in cross-platform and slightly comedic digital combat, social acceptance came knocking via his head set.

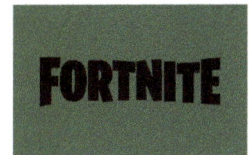

FORTNITE

The digital playground literally transcended the physical and enabled Laurence to assert a social status amongst his peers that made the rest of his time at that school a good deal more enjoyable - and I'll wager he learned more as a result too.

And that, dear reader, was me converted. I am a believer in the social power of gaming. These digital vistas that entice and enthrall are no longer a vacuous wasteland inhabited by maladjusted young men in darkened rooms. They are an explosion of collaboration, colour and conversation. I never thought I'd say this, but games can be really very good for our children - and they know it. And that is why gaming is the biggest, strongest, fastest growing pillar of the children's entertainment world.

The key components of all games -- whether card games, board games, playground games or video games -- are universal: goals, rules, strategy, challenge and interaction. And that's the key word, isn't it? "Interaction".

I don't need to tell you how popular gaming is - but let's take a moment to remind ourselves...

In 2008, 79% of boys and 43% of girls would play video games after school. Today 96% of all children play video games. I reckon it's more like 99%, but the stats say what they say. Whichever way you look at it, more than 9 out of 10 children are playing video games - and they do it because they are programmed to.

Glenn Carstens, Unsplash

Let me explain.

Effective socialisation in our species is arguably the most important aspect of our development. Social development along with Physical, Emotional and Cognitive Development is a building block for life. Effective Socialisation is also one of the core need states that we consider at Kids Industries whenever developing product, digital or physical, for young people. Childhood is perhaps the most socialised time of our lives - you're literally locked up with 30 other people for 8 hours a day. Relationships are forged and broken with a startling velocity and, as in all social groupings, it is shared experience that binds us or parts us.

According to Bartle's Taxonomy of Player Types -- which is based on a 1996 paper by games researcher Richard Bartle -- players can be categorised into four groups: Achievers, Explorers, Socialisers and Killers, with socialisers being the most common. In fact, 80

percent of gamers are socialisers. So, if Socialisers are the mainstay of gamers, and childhood is the most socially focused time of our lives, then it seems no surprise at all why gaming is the entertainment of choice for 9 out of ten under 18s.

Back in my day (always wanted to write that) you could all sit around and take turns with the two Atari 2600 or the SNES controllers - but you all had to be in the same place to socialise. Now we're in an entirely new world facilitated by a new generation of hardware; the cross-platform, internet-driven world of live conversation with friends, doing stuff together, whilst being physically apart. And with games, you always do, you don't just watch. Unless you happen to be spectating at an eSports stadium or glued to a Twitch stream, that is - but even these more passive activities offer opportunities for socialisation and community building.

For children, games are a conduit through which they extend their playtime shenanigans. From chat to party modes, interactive representations of others are accepted and considered a valid extension of the self. The lines between the physical and digital worlds are becoming increasingly blurred, and young people are perfectly at home with it. We are already in Ready Player One. Even before the pandemic, this was an obvious and charted trend - the Metaverse was coming. Now it's here and maybe it arrived a little earlier than expected.

Robert Collins, Unsplash

I believe in play - real play, outside running about with your mates play. Or imagining play with action figures. Play is the work of the child; it is what they need to do to become who they are destined to be. And this last year there's not been enough of that play - but at least they've been able to explore the virtual world with their friends - and perhaps to do so without the watchful eyes of parents, to fulfil that need for autonomy, has, at least in part, been satisfied by gaming.

Music was the shared experience that defined the first tribes of youth culture, providing the growing-up milestones for Boomers and Generation Xers. But it is gaming that now provides the nexus for the shared experiences of GenZ and, more importantly, Generation Alpha. Gaming in 2021 corrals so much of a child's life. It's IP, it's play, it's friendship. They invest their time and themselves in this miraculous digital panacea and it is through this investment that friendships and communities are built. Communities build culture - and culture gives us the framework for effective socialisation. Although they have been apart for an entire year, they've never been more together.

It's all quite beautiful really.

Denisse Leon, Unsplash

Nicjolas J Leclerc, Unsplash

THE BOY IN THE DRESS

Diversity and Inclusivity are important to young people and they are
more accepting of difference than previous generations. We've come a
long way in portraying difference, whether it's skin colour or disability.
However, there's still some way to go to diverse audiences recognising
themselves on screen, and the devil is in the detail.

Sharon McCutcheon, Unsplash

CHILDREN'S DIVERSITY AND REPRESENTATION – NOT JUST SKIN DEEP

BY MARCUS RYDER

—

#FirstTimeISawMe

A few years ago the hashtag #FirstTimeISawMe started trending on social media.

The hashtag was part of an awareness campaign by Netflix focusing on diversity and inclusion. It highlighted seminal TV moments and characters when people from under-represented groups first experienced their own reality and personality accurately portrayed on screen, enabling them to feel included and "seen".

The hashtag primarily focused on ethnicity but soon grew into a wider discussion on issues around gender, sexuality and disability. The social media conversations vividly illustrated what it meant to people to feel represented for the first time. Tweets, Facebook updates and Instagram pictures all built up, giving deeply personal accounts that proved how important on-screen diversity is for people.

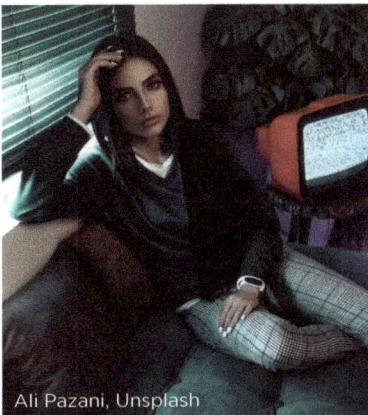

Ali Pazani, Unsplash

However, while much of the debate this stimulated centred on the "ISeeMe" part of the hashtag, which was all about diversity and representation, there was little debate about the first part of the hashtag; "FirstTime".

Considering we all watched television as children this was implicitly a debate about representation (or lack thereof) in children's programming - whether people realised it or not. If the first time people "saw themselves" was in adult programming this must surely mean they did not see themselves represented throughout their childhood. Conversely, if they cited examples

65

from children's programmes or family programmes this was a powerful endorsement of representation in programmes aimed at children.

Interestingly the examples that people gave of the #FirstTimeISawMe were rarely about their race, gender, disability or sexuality alone. It was always a lot more complex and nuanced. If one looks at ethnicity for example, while black people usually gave an example of a black character for the first time they saw themselves, it was rarely the actual first time they had seen a black character on TV. Ethnicity alone did not guarantee that people felt "seen" or saw themselves in the character.

People's race plays an important part of them seeing themselves reflected on-screen but it is just one part of a far larger whole. This complexity is almost taken for granted in representation of white characters for a white audience... no one expects a white child to identify with every white character they see on screen. Obviously a raft of other factors come into play such as gender, class, regionality and more. However, when I speak to people about on-screen black representation with senior television executives this complexity is often overlooked.

Yet it is crucial.

I remember the first time I "saw myself" on television.

John John was a small black boy with an afro counting to twenty with Herry Monster on *Sesame Street*. For a small black boy living in a predominately white London suburb, I had found my place in the world. It also didn't hurt that my full name is actually Jon-Marcus and my family often called me "Jon Bon", it was close enough to "John John".

Sesame Street

There were other black children on *Sesame Street* but only John John was me. His afro, his age, his name, and the fact he loved counting all added up to enable me to see myself.

I saw my own 5-year-old son go through the same experience a few months ago.

He is an avid watcher of the CBeebies series *Go Jetters*, a cartoon with four intrepid adventurers guided by a disco loving unicorn, who rescue global treasures from being destroyed by the evil Grandmaster Glitch. The four adventurers are of different races, three of the four are boys and one is a girl.

Go Jetters

One of the characters, Lars, is black. But for the whole first series my son, who is also black, did not seem to notice him any more than any of the other characters. If anything, he seemed to identify most with the unicorn.

Then, in series two something interesting happened.

Throughout the first series the four adventurers wear one-piece uniforms with hoods covering their hair. I have never produced animation but I assume it is a lot cheaper to have characters that don't have hair. But with a successful first series the creators started to do a few scenes with the adventurers' hair exposed.

All of a sudden, my son saw Lar's curly hair and that moment of recognition was almost electric.

At five-years-old my son does not have a strong understanding of race, quite understandably and possibly thankfully. But currently he seems to mediate his own race, and any racial differences and similarities he has with friends, through his hair texture.

The second he saw Lar's hair he identified with the black character. He did not identify through the different skin tones of the different characters. His perception of self and (I suspect) race is seen through the prism of hair not melanin.

Go Jetters

Representation matters and my son saw himself.

Why do I bring this up?

It is because when we discuss diversity and race we often see it through categories recognised through our adult perspective. If we were to objectively assess the on-screen diversity of *Go Jetters* series one vs series two nothing had changed: Four different characters, one of them is black.

But for my son, and perhaps for countless other children it went from four characters of different hues to suddenly seeing themselves.

This also illustrates a point I've made before that too often diversity is seen as an end in itself - however diversity is just a means to an end.

If diversity was the end goal *Go Jetters* accomplished its mission in series one, when in reality it only hit the mark (as far as my son is concerned) in series two.

If our goal is to ensure that children can personally connect to the characters in the story and feel positive about themselves, we need to ensure that we explore how children racially identify themselves, not how we (as adults) identify them. There is literally no point in getting the brown paintboxes out if skin colour is not how they identify themselves. Put another way, we can't just stop at the brown paintbox.

The same goes for any number of identifiers, from accents to family structures, and from disabilities to genders.

Identity is multi-layered.

Which brings me to my main point. If we are to achieve effective on-screen diversity that connects with our children then better representation behind the camera is essential.

Having grown up as a black child and now raising a black boy gives me a completely different perspective of what "genuine representation" looks like and what small points need to be brought out.

For example, before my son became an avid *Go Jetters* fan he loved *Bing* (an animated bunny who lives in a neighbourhood with other anthropomorphic friends and their carers). Again, there is little doubt that the creators of *Bing* are sensitive to issues of diversity with many of the characters seeming to have different accents. But in all the episodes I have watched (there are a lot - so I will not pretend to have watched them all) not once did I see *Bing*, or any of his friends, have "non-Western" food. Food is often a central theme in children's stories and in a wider context food is often one of the easiest ways to convey different cultures. And yet representations of food frequently become exclusionary for children of different ethnicities and cultures. Samosas, jollof rice, and jerk chicken are relegated to non-experiences or are exoticised in "special" episodes which primarily focus on ethnicity.

Bing

Irrespective of how many black or brown characters directors and storytellers create, if children view their identity through food the nominal racial diversity will do little to help children connect with these characters and "see themselves".

Chinh Le Duc, Unsplash

Similarly, knives, forks and spoons in children's cartoons seem to be a given. I have never seen a parent serving food with chopsticks or children characters using them despite the fact that by some estimates a third of the world uses chopsticks on a daily basis. From Ethiopia to Indonesia, millions of people mark family time or special occasions with shared food, in many cases eaten with hands.

If we want children to recognise themselves we need to constantly strive to normalise different cultural experiences and recognise that ethnicity goes way beyond simple signifiers of skin colour.

Another example is shoes. I have lived in Asia for just over five years, first in China, briefly in Thailand, and currently in Malaysia. In all those years I have never seen anybody wear shoes in their house. When I visit another home, I am expected to take off my shoes before entering and may be offered slippers to use inside. And yet, like the example of chopsticks, I cannot recall ever seeing a child take their shoes off in children's cartoons when they go into someone's house.

Jakob Owens, Unsplash

In the simple act of keeping their shoes on a character goes from being an Asian character that Asian children may be able to relate to, to yet another character who simply has different skin colour. This is of course despite the best of intentions the director behind the camera might have had to represent a multicultural audience.

Cine-Direktor Films

The examples of how we can undermine our best intentions are too numerous to cite and almost impossible for someone who is not immersed in that culture to recognise. Which is why diversity behind the camera – and specifically in editorial positions - is so important. It is the small nuances that can make all the difference. What kind of food would the character eat? Why is their hair important? What do they do when they enter a house? How should they address their parents? Would their grandparents live in the house or nearby? Do they eat with their hands or chopsticks or knives and forks?

It is literally too exhausting if we have to think through every one of these questions consciously, and elongate the list too. Which is why ultimately you need content creators from a range of backgrounds who do not have to think about these issues consciously but for whom it is simply second nature if they try to represent their own culture that they draw on their own childhood for reference.

If I have not yet been able to convince you of the importance of diversity behind the camera when it comes to kids' shows I have one last point:

One is not enough.

If we accept that our identities are multi-layered with things such as race or gender only playing a part, then the idea that a single black character or female character will be able to capture all the representational needs of children of that gender or ethnicity runs contrary to common sense. And yet all too often we still see the single black or single female character in a larger group majority white or male group.

Returning to my experience of "seeing myself" for the first time in John John in *Sesame Street* it is important to remember that Sesame Street had a range of different black characters. I didn't "see myself" in Sally (another black child in Sesame Street) for example.

We must break free of the idea that diversity and representation can be achieved through a single character in a story any more than we think every white child can identify with every white character.

Diversity is not the same as representation and is only part of a far larger whole.

To achieve true representation in front of the camera which children can relate to, we need true diversity and representation behind the camera.

If the hashtag #FirstTimeISawMe was able to open up a whole discussion about on-screen diversity, maybe those of us working in the media industry need to start a new hashtag #FirstTimeISawMeWorking. Now that would be real progress!

DIVERSITY IN CHILDREN'S BOOKS

SARAH DOYLE

—

During the Summer of 2020 I had the pleasure of producing a session in the 'Inclusivity Now' strand of the Children's Media Conference; working with the organisation Inclusive Minds we produced a (hopefully) thought provoking and interesting video focusing on Intentional Inclusion in the world of children's literature. The key areas spoken about were: reflecting on personal experiences, professional practices, and cultural shifts.

My own background is in design, so I not only want to discuss the key learnings from our session. I also want to explore the relationship between diversity, accessibility and design in the children's publishing space - and how design can open up the world of reading to as many children as possible. I want to discuss some of the key points that were made in our session, and also look at some features of book design that open up the world of reading to as many children as possible.

WHY ARE BOOKS IMPORTANT?

Books are one of the earliest forms of media that children are exposed to, and even at a young age they are already subconsciously looking for representation. Fiction allows children to see themselves represented, and to interact with characters and worlds that feel relatable to the child in real life but fiction also explores the escapism of fantasy and adventure. However, it can be difficult to relate to a story if a child doesn't feel they are being represented fairly or sometimes

Jerry Wang, Unsplash

even at all. These early role models are already shaping a child's perspective and future expectations of certain people and cultures, so a negative representation or an inaccurate one can warp their interpretation or understanding - or cause a child to disassociate from the narrative if they find themselves or their background misrepresented.

With regards to disabilities specifically, there are very few role models that are included within children's literature, and even fewer are represented in a positive light. Often these under-represented characters are given small roles or portrayed using stereotypes. There are a few positive examples of disability inclusion from authors such as Michael Morpurgo in *"The Ghost of Grania O'Malley"*, or Jacqueline Wilson in *"The Worry Website and Penny Joelson: I Have No Secrets"*. This representation is shifting, albeit very slowly.

REPRESENTATION MATTERS

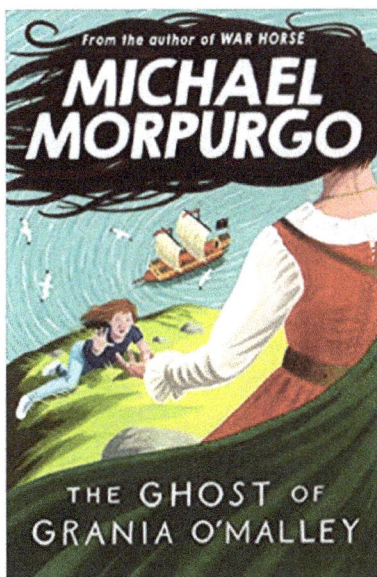

Authors have a responsibility to ensure that any depictions of any disabilities, cultures or experiences are handled sensitively and genuinely. For example, they need to ask themselves "is this character a token diverse cast member, or is this a genuine representation of who they are?" This is a really key point, because this will shape whether or not the character feels like a stereotype or a true reflection of the person. Capturing true authenticity requires lots of research and connecting with the audience you are trying to write about. The subtle differences are in the nuances and in the language itself, which can only be learned from people within those communities.

There needs to be a careful but considered balance between making sure people from these groups are able to tell their stories but equally do not feel pressured to educate fellow authors and audiences. "The Burden of Representation" is the sense that people from marginalised groups are expected to tell stories directly about their backgrounds and experiences. There can be a pressure then to educate people actively and constantly which is an unfair expectation.

There is no substitute for lived experience, so there also needs to be a wider conversation about how to increase opportunities for a more diverse array of children's authors. Whether this starts early in the education system, with making literature accessible for more children, school visits from established authors, and supporting aspiring young authors of all ages with mentorships, or publishers providing grants for higher education to ensure the right voices are heard.

DIGITAL DESIGN INTEGRATION

So how can design factor into making sure children can both access books and feel represented by them? As I have mentioned, my background is in design, and I have always had an interest in User Experience (UX) and user journeys as they are a key part of creating a well thought-out project. But beyond the basic usability I started to wonder if some of the publishing principles mentioned above could also be applied to design products and experiences in order to be more inclusive and accessible to a larger range of children who want to read.

I think it's worth quickly discussing the difference between Accessible Design and Inclusive Design as both are relevant and important in the next part. Accessible Design very simply means that everyone should be able to use the product; when it is built, is it possible for everyone to use it fully? For books this could include a large print edition, localisation, braille copies or audio book integration support. Inclusive Design is subtly different, as it takes the accessible product and asks does everyone want to use this product? Does the product

Alireza Atari, Unsplash

feel authentic and does the user feel comfortable using it? This covers a lot of what we have previously spoken about with respect to the content of the book. Children's books should always feel authentic, and should be a true representation of the groups or cultures featured. Combining elements of both of these design principles is key.

"While Accessible Design cares only that everyone can hear your message, Inclusive Design asks you to consider your message itself."

ACCESSIBLE DESIGN

Emily Wade, Unsplash

Traditionally children who are visually impaired rely much more on adaptive displays and audio features. Most of us are familiar with the option to scale up text on electronic devices like Kindles or iPads. Accessibility options often use audio integration either to read along or to enhance the narrative, like a podcast or soundscape. Features can also reduce the input required to use the product (for example swiping to change a page) which can help any child with mobility or coordination issues. Designing for children requires simple consistent User Interface and features that are intuitive, and use a visual hierarchy.

The great news is a lot of digital platforms have flexible accessibility support features. However, this is not standardised yet, and children can be "penalised" by these products often being more expensive, published a while after the original, or difficult to get a hold of. Digital formats are opening up the world of children's books to new readers all the time, and whilst there is still room for these platforms to improve, there can be no doubt of the positive impact these new platforms are having on reaching new readers all over the world.

CELEBRATE OUR DIFFERENCES

Differences are a part of everyday life. These should be embraced, celebrated and reflected in the pages of books. For children, it is incredibly empowering to see stories and experiences they can identify with in the pages of literature, to embrace their identity and cultures, and to normalise their own life experiences.

KEY TAKE AWAYS

- Ensure you work for authenticity early on in the process: capture the nuances, do lots of research and talk to the community you're writing about.

- Amplify marginalised people's voices: they deserve to be heard. There's no real substitute for someone's own lived experience: we don't want to speak for them.

- Differences are a part of everyday life, they should be embraced, celebrated and reflected in the pages of books.

- Combine inclusive and accessible digital design principles for the best experiences.

REPRESENTATION MATTERS DEEPLY AND OTHER DISRUPTIONS IN DISTRIBUTION

BY TOM VAN WAVEREN

—

2020 was very unusual in many ways, for the world and for the media industry. As it turned out, it was also unusual for me, as it was to become the last of my 15 years as CEO of Cake Entertainment, an independent company specialising in development, production, distribution and financing of kid's properties.

As children's programme makers, 2020 made us rethink how we tell stories, how our industry functions and what the brave new world of content is likely to look like in years ahead. We did not only rethink these matters because the world in lockdown, which we slowly learned to navigate, probably gave us more time to think than we were used to, but mainly because the consequences of a few key events gave us the opportunity to reflect on what should be the foundations of our industry from here on forward.

Hair Love

The first such key event, for me, was *Hair Love* winning the Oscar for Best Animated Short Film on February 9th 2020. Written by Matthew A Cherry and co-produced by Karen Rupert Toliver of Sony Pictures Animation, it is the story of an African American dad helping his young daughter do her hair before picking her mother up from hospital together. As co-producer Karen Rupert Toliver said in her acceptance speech, 'representation matters deeply, especially in cartoons, because in cartoons that's when we first see our movies that empower us and shape our lives and think about how we see our world', and I challenge anyone in our industry to disagree with that very important statement.

The fact that HBO Max commissioned a series based on the *Hair Love* short, while other networks followed suit with diverse commissions throughout 2020, shows that it was merely riding the crest of a wave that has been building momentum over the last few years. Naturally, the protest around the death of George Floyd certainly helped shift the focus as well, but the ground swell was there.

The streaming platforms, and Netflix in particular, deserve credit for being at the forefront of the focus on diverse and authentic storytelling from all corners of the world and sections of our communities, which they have been supporting well ahead of *Hair Love*. The Netflix original *Mama K's Team* that Cake is currently in production on, is a great example of this trend, as it was created by Malenga Mulendema from Zambia. This animated action comedy has four black teenage girls in the lead of a story world based in Lusaka, capital of Zambia, with Cape Town based animation studio Triggerfish as initiator of the project and lead creative studio, and was developed and commissioned well ahead of 2020.

Mamma K's Team

Not only have all children's specialty networks been commissioning much more diverse content in 2020 than they ever have before, they have also made multiple key editorial and corporate appointments within their organisations, and created new roles, to secure this diversity perspective and focus going forward. This means that telling diverse and authentic stories is not only important, it has now become an attractive business opportunity as well, and that is excellent news for all of us.

Seeing African, Asian, Latin American, African American and many other diverse stories being commissioned in animated films and series will enrich the story experiences of our audience, but most importantly, it will greatly improve the chances for children across the world to see themselves represented on screen, represented as the heroes and protagonists of the stories that reflect their own lives and not just that of others, and that is a BIG win.

kidscreen

Fast forward to the next key event, the week of March 16th 2020, when our whole industry was set up to work remotely and we were forced to re-think how we live and work. We discussed at Kidscreen Summit in Miami, just a month earlier, that we were missing a certain number of our Asian counterparts, but most of us expected them to be back in Cannes for the major industry market Mip TV in April, once they had dealt with the nuisance of Covid. The rest as they say, is history.

Traditionally, being a distributor has meant traveling to events, year-round, and going to see our clients where they live and work. For 30 years I travelled around Europe and the world and was away from home 2 to 3 times each month. We used to say to our clients that there was always at least one event around the world every month of the year that Cake was attending to present our content to the world. This was simply not an option in 2020. Instead, I, as well as the rest of the Cake team, stayed at home for 12 months in a row, which I enjoyed a lot more than I had expected - the not traveling part that is.

Consequently, we have had to re-invent our approach and adapt to building and maintaining relationships by digital interaction only. We found out that it is a lot easier to keep in contact with existing partners than it is to get to know new ones in this new reality, but both have been an explicit focus of the Cake team.

What we have learned, as all our tentpole industry calendar moments went digital one after the other, is that digital versions of such events are hard to organize. However, it is extremely important to keep certain weeks in the calendar when we, as an industry, focus to catch up with a broader group than the people we are actively engaged with in the day to day.

We also learned that if you are not forced to have all your meetings within three or four days in a cramped conference venue, you can plan your meetings over a two to three-week period and have longer conversations, to make up for the lack of live interaction. And, it flattens the curve a little and makes it easier to follow up on meetings as they unfold, instead of coming home to a pile of such work after pitching at international markets.

On a more micro level, we learned that there are many different video conferencing applications and all of them work differently, and none make pitching the same as in person, even if you can share your screen and figure out how your videos can play fluently. Not having eye contact with the individuals you are pitching to makes you oddly aware of your own voice and what you are saying, which favours well-rehearsed and written-out pitches to the more improvised style that we were used to before. But hey, we made it work.

And finally, there was never as much binging as over last year. We were all hungry for content, the children's audience was very much part of this, and subscriber numbers for SVOD (Subscription Video on Demand) platforms rose to new record heights. It means that the change from linear to on demand viewing has further accelerated and we are still trying to figure out the exact impact this will have on our key clients and business models.

So, as I figure out what I will do in 2021 and the world slowly starts functioning more like before, we are still and will remain in an industry where children's content is a booming business and one that has raised the bar of diversity and authenticity, so let's face that challenge and embrace that opportunity together.

KEEP THE ASPIDISTRA FLYING

Children aren't the only ones with remarkable resilience. We grownups can adapt to sudden change too. What happens when a global pandemic shuts the world down? The show must go on, no matter what.

Annie Spratt, Unsplash

ANIMATION IN LOCKDOWN

BY JULIAN SCOTT

In the final weeks before the initial lockdown in March 2020, I was preparing for an inbound delegation of animation executives from the west coast of the US and Canada. There were rumblings around the world about the pandemic, and people were becoming nervous about the effect it might have; if one person showed symptoms, should the whole studio be closed for two weeks? Then BAM, on March 23rd, everything stopped, and everything shut.

Avel Chuklanov, Unsplash

The Covid pandemic had a massive effect on television and film production across the UK and tested the media industry's resource and entrepreneurial spirit. Within days of lockdown, live-action production had all but ceased, and due to its inherent close contact, working practices looked unlikely to start up again for some time. However, animation was back up and running within a couple of weeks and at near full capacity. The very nature of the animation process meant that staff could work remotely, and several facilities had been trialling this way of working for a few weeks in case of such a crisis. New technologies were developed or enhanced to facilitate this. One London outfit had moved to cloud-based technology, meaning that the move to working remotely was almost instantaneous.

Kensuke's Kingdom Ltd.

A new way of working had begun; Hollywood studios obsessed with their IP being leaked had to accept that the usual security procedures had to go by the wayside if the films were to be finished. Major features were being created on kitchen tables and in spare rooms across the country, and broadcasters and SVODs began to notice. The airwaves and downloads still had to be fed; people were at home and turning more and more to the TV for comfort. Within a month or so, animation studios were beginning to quietly confirm that commissions were picking up and not just from the more traditional children's channels. Commercials producers were being asked if ad campaigns could be animated, Hollywood feature films were brought forward and released online rather than through cinemas. The animation sector started to be taken more seriously by other screen industries and noticed by commissioners and financiers as a viable alternative to live-action.

Although the sector bounced back quickly from lockdown and was at 90% capacity within a few weeks, other issues arose from the situation, as the pandemic continued and the lockdown carried on. Individuals' mental well-being became a concern. Many junior animators are young and often live in smaller, less than ideal accommodation, sometimes shared, which means they can spend long periods isolated from other people. The collaborative and inclusive nature of a studio

Andrew Neel, Unsplash

and the water-cooler moments disappeared. For many, the studio wasn't just a place of work; it was where friends met and talked, careers were launched, and talent was spotted.

Paddington, Season 2 © MARMALADE FILMS LIMITED - MASCARET FILMS SAS 2019

Mentoring, inspiration, training, and just keeping an eye on your team became much harder. As someone commented, "You can't schedule a Zoom for spontaneity."

The secondary effect of the pandemic is that it has counteracted some of the impacts of Brexit, in that safe, productive, remote working

practices allowed studios to tap into European talent who can no longer quickly move across the Channel to work on projects in one of the numerous animation hubs in the UK. However, there is an obvious loss in doing that as those labour costs won't qualify for the UK tax credit.

So, what of the future? The industry has never been busier; recent data shows that year on year, the amount being spent on animation in the UK has continued to rise despite the pandemic. So, should the industry be celebrating? Obviously, but with some caution – there are

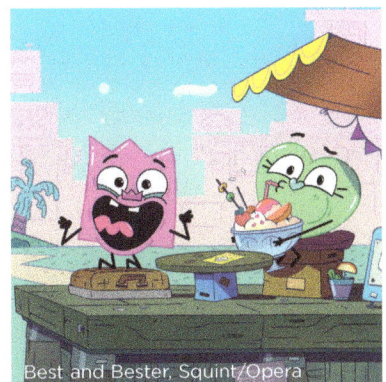
Best and Bester, Squint/Opera

still hurdles to be jumped. Despite some negativity, our tax credit remains one of the best in the world. It may not have the best headline percentage, but when you drill down it is very competitive and ranks in the top three incentives in the world. Some territories have used the Covid situation to rush through 'emergency' measure to increase their gross incentives. However, many are capped, there can be long lead times before receiving the investment and there are other restrictions that are not immediately obvious. Lobbying by stakeholders continues in an attempt to convince the Treasury to increase our overall animation tax credit. One large London-based studio believes an increase of 5% in the credit could treble their turnover.

Paddington, Season 2

Another challenge will be skills. The increase in remote working and the use of non-UK talent remains an option but it's not ideal in the long term. If the relaxation of Covid working restrictions becomes a long-term reality, there will be a natural desire to return to collegiate working. But at the moment, we simply don't have enough animators and other key talents to fill the seats. ScreenSkills and other organisations, together with the studios, are working hard to address this. Still, it won't be a quick fix, and we have a relatively short period to seize the opportunity.

For some time, the main desire of the animation sector has been to be taken seriously and recognised as a creative business. Out of adversity, that opportunity has arisen. If the industry receives the support and backing for it to remain competitive, it will continue to grow and be successful on the global stage. ⊙

YAKKA DEE! PRODUCTION THROUGH THE PANDEMIC.

LOTTE ELWELL

—

Yakka Dee! is a mixed media live action and animation series that encourages children to talk. Each episode focusses on one word and an animated chatterbox. Dee and friends take us on a journey around that word, so that by the end of the episode children will have learnt the word with a lot of laughs along the way. In the Autumn of 2019, we went into production on our 4th and 5th series for CBeebies. By now a well-honed machine, *Yakka Dee*! Series 4 + 5 would run like clockwork. Or so we thought...

In February 2020, I was at Kidscreen in Miami – a huge global children's media summit at which *Yakka Dee*! had been nominated for an award... In a massive Miami hotel chocked to the brim full of thousands of people from the industry, we had no idea what was about to hit us. Back at home, series 4 + 5 of *Yakka Dee*! was in full swing. By mid-March, we were three weeks into shooting with another seven to go when the pandemic hit and our world was turned upside down.

It seems strange now to think we hadn't seen it coming, but no one had. In the weeks leading up to the first lockdown in the UK, we had started to worry... could this affect us? Or was it all going to blow over? No-one seemed to know. We were advised by the BBC to keep up-to-date with Public Health England announcements, which we duly did and we sought advice from our health and safety advisors but no-one was clear on the best way to proceed and at that stage there was very little solid advice – not even from the government.

Then suddenly it was upon us – like an avalanche! The Monday before our fourth studio week, the government urged people to work from home and avoid large groups. They advised against non-essential travel and contact with others and included pregnant

women in their at-risk groups. One of the Series Producers on *Yakka Dee!* was recently pregnant, so she was now confined to working from home. One of the live action directors had a family member who was displaying symptoms. She was confined to home. The situation started to feel serious, but there was still no instruction from the government to stop working and still no-one really knew what was going on. As a small company we stood to lose a lot if we decided to stop production with no direction to do so, so we planned to continue, taking all the precautions we could.

By Wednesday, it was announced all schools would close on Friday. Woah! Big setback... As a company we are passionate about flexible working to allow parents back to work, and most of the members of our team are parents. How will they work and home-school their children? Will councils let our performer children still come to the studio? The situation really hit home!

By Thursday, we were in crisis talks. The area our studio is based in has one of the largest numbers of covid cases in the UK. But still the government hadn't told us to stop and as the situation stood, we could be held liable by the BBC for not fulfilling our contract and delivering the series on time.

Friday – one of the worst days of my life! I'm in tears on the phone to our BBC Executive Producer, who kindly did her best to reassure us we were unlikely to be held to our delivery dates. Despite lockdown not being announced, we made the decision it was not safe to film the following week and had to ring around all our contributors to tell them the news, and our entire production team to tell them they now had no work – for an indefinite amount of time.

Monday 23rd March – finally nationwide lockdown was announced and whilst this might not seem like good news, it filled me with a sense of relief that this was at last out of our hands.

But, what then? *Yakka Dee!* is a mixed media series – half live action and half animation. The live action was, for now at least, on hold. But the animation side of things could keep running and our animators – Mighty

Studios (based in Mexico) had plenty to be getting on with. So – in order not to extend our schedule any further than necessary (because that meant extra budget, as well as late delivery times), we decided to keep that arm of production running. In between home-schooling and struggling to get our heads in order after the extreme shock of what had just happened, we carried on. A week into lockdown myself and my family were struck down with covid. Luckily it affected us fairly mildly and whilst I felt rough and strange and couldn't taste or smell anything for a couple of weeks, I was still able to work.

We continued like this for a month or so, getting as much of the animation side of things done as possible, whilst beginning to re-work our entire schedule to accommodate the current situation. First task – work out when we needed to start filming again in order to keep the animation side of production running. We worked out we had until July. If we could start filming again in July, the animators would keep a steady flow of work going and we could deliver both series a mere month overdue, despite live action production being paused for four months! But would this be possible? Only time and information on covid infection rates would tell…

As we entered June, we began to hit crunch time. If we were going to re-start production before the end of July and keep the whole series running, we would need to start sourcing new locations, contributors and doing all our set up by the end of the month. We decided to take a leap of faith and go for it. We thought we'd have a window over the summer where production

is more possible, as we could film more outdoors and that would really aid social distancing and lessen any risk of spread. We also suspected the pandemic may take a turn for the worse in the Autumn when weather would begin to turn colder.

We had to make quite a few adjustments to our ways of working to accommodate the 'new normal' and ensure we were working in a safe way: We cut down our filming team to a bare minimum. The rest of the team would work from home, do all set up and preparation for our shoots to enable us to cut down time needed between shoot weeks. This meant we could fit in everything we needed to do before infection rates started to rise again. They also acted as a 'back up' team, in case anyone on the shooting team displayed symptoms or was asked to self-isolate.

We changed our contributors so that we only had children from one family at any one time. Before we always had several children at a time so they could give each other confidence and we could swap contributors in and out, but this was no longer possible unless the children were part of the same family. So, we sought out more sibling groups. This had the wonderful effect of actually showing a really special relationship on screen.

We aimed to film as much as possible in outdoor locations and find as many locations as possible where the public wouldn't be present but where we'd have plenty of space and the right facilities to ensure safety of our team and contributors.

Obviously, we had to completely re-visit our health and safety procedures and risk assessments and ensure the whole team were trained in the new ways of working safely. Regular temperature checks, mask wearing, hand sanitising, social-distancing, cleaning down props, equipment and surfaces became the norm. We had a rigorous set of health and safety procedures and followed them to the letter. One of the most challenging areas was props and costumes, which we had to ensure weren't handled by anyone other than the child or family using them. Our brilliant team rose to the challenge.

Lotte Elwell

Another challenge was to make sure we made our contributors felt absolutely comfortable in these strange, new and potentially less friendly surroundings. The team worked tirelessly to do this, putting huge amounts of effort into making the children feel welcome and at home – despite needing to keep their distance.

We were careful enough, and fortunate enough, to get through our entire filming period with no covid cases until our final week. The daughter of our DOP tested positive after a school friend was found to be positive. Luckily, with all our safety measures in place to ensure team members were not in close contact, it was only the DOP who was unable to complete the shoot and we had someone else on standby to step into his shoes and complete the shoot as scheduled.

With the shoot out of the way, everyone breathed a huge sigh of relief as shortly after that, covid cases started to seriously rise and the situation became much more precarious. Next challenge – complete all our post-production and animation from home. By then, it was no longer possible for either our post-production team or our animators to be working from

their studios and all the team needed to re-locate to their homes to continue. Obviously, this was more possible for post-production and animation but also took much more time, as it involved new edits and dubs being sent out to be reviewed after every set of notes. Not to mention home broadband speeds leaving us despairing on many occasions!

Finally, through three lockdowns and a massive world-changing event, thanks to a hugely dedicated team in the UK and Mexico, we completed 40 more episodes of *Yakka Dee*! We sincerely hope the next 40 will be a simpler process, but whatever happens, we know we'll pull together and make them as high quality, engaging and fun as ever. Bring it on!

CHILDREN'S BOOKS BRAVE THE PANDEMIC

PHILIP STONE

—

Standfirst: Helped by surging sales of home-schooling titles, the children's book market has navigated the pandemic relatively unscathed. Data from Nielsen Book Research reports uplifts across numerous genres, that helped the popularity of titles both old and new.

When bricks and mortar booksellers closed their doors in March last year, few in the book industry would have been brave enough to predict that printed book sales in the UK would grow in 2020. But that is exactly what happened.

Nielsen Book's estimate of physical book sales in 2020, based on a blend of data from our Total Consumer Market panel of more than 6,500 UK book retail outlets, and consumer survey data, reveals that 202m printed books were bought in the UK in 2020, up 5% against 2019, with sales totalling £1.76bn, up 6% year on year.

In a year of severe disruption unfortunately Nielsen Book was not immune to COVID-19's effects. The pandemic impacted our ability to report UK book sales data during lockdown periods. That said, the 36 weeks of reportable point-of-sale data we have from 2020 totals more than 140m units and almost £1.3bn — so not an insignificant amount.

Data from our Total Consumer Market panel during non-lockdown periods last year also revealed year-on-year growth across numerous genres, including popular psychology and self-help, crime fiction, arts and crafts, and food and drink. In addition, there was substantial growth across numerous children's genres, most notably within the non-fiction sector — an area of focus in our contribution to last year's Children's Media Yearbook.

Our survey: *Impact of COVID-19 on the UK Book Consumer* published in July last year revealed that 54% of respondents said they had spent more time "helping children with homework" during the first lockdown than during pre-pandemic times, while just 4% reported doing less. As such, it is perhaps no surprise to find that sales of Reference and Home Learning titles enjoyed

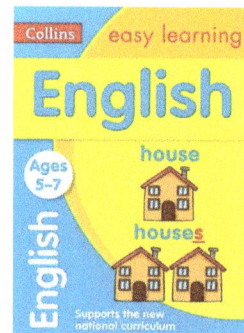

a substantial uplift in 2020, with the *Collins Easy Learning* range proving particularly popular. For many parents across the UK, home learning workbooks were definitely "essential" purchases last year, even if the UK government deemed bookshops not "essential" at all.

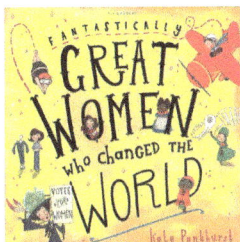

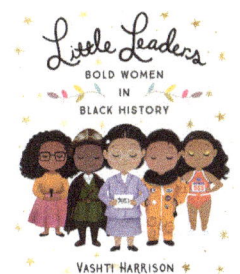

Maths workbooks and spelling and handwriting guides were not the only titles in the children's and young adult non-fiction sector to prove popular. Other sub-categories that enjoyed buoyant sales included: history, spurred by the success of **Kate Pankhurst's** *Fantastically Great Women* and **Vashti Harrison's** *Little Leaders* ranges; biography, boosted by the huge popularity of **Maria Isabel Sanchez Vegara's** *Little People, BIG DREAMS* series (books on **David Attenborough**, **Captain Tom Moore** and **Rosa Parks** were the bestsellers in 2020); science, thanks in part to **Dr Adam Kay's** smash hit, *Kay's Anatomy*, and Usborne's ever-popular *See Inside* range; and personal and social issues, with **Matthew Syed's** *You Are Awesome* and *Dare to Be You* proving among the more popular in a sector that continues to reflect how mental health taboos are being broken.

Sales of books for younger audiences also grew last year. 36% of respondents to our *Impact of COVID-19 on the UK Book Consumers* survey said they read to, or with, children more during the pandemic compared to pre-pandemic times, with just 7% reporting that they do it less.

Classic characters continue to dominate a sector that relies on purchasing by parents and grandparents. **Julia Donaldson** titles took 10 spots in the list of the top 20 bestselling children's pre-school books last year, with her *The Smeds and the Smoos* the overall number one. **Craig Smith's** *The Wonky Donkey*, first published in 2010, was also among the top 20 bestsellers of the year, enjoying an impressive longevity after a video of a grandmother laughing hysterically as she read the book went viral in 2018.

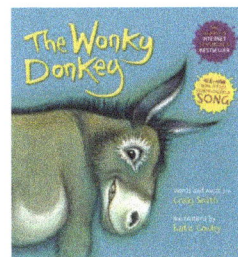

Its endurance, though, is nothing compared to four other titles in the top 20: Rod Campbell's *Dear Zoo* (first published in 1982), **Eric Hill's** *Where's Spot?* (1980), **Eric Carle's** *The Very Hungry Caterpillar* (1969) and **Judith Kerr's** *The Tiger Who Came to Tea* (1968).

Children's and young adult fiction sales also rose in 2020. **David Walliams** remains comfortably the bestselling writer in the sector, exemplified by the fact his *Code Name Bananas* (published in November last year), *Slime* (published in April 2020) and *The World's Worst Parents* (published in July 2020) were the top three bestselling titles overall in the sector. All three were hardbacks. The bestselling children's and young adult fiction paperback of 2020? That title went to **J K Rowling's** *Harry Potter and the Philosopher's Stone*. Although 2020 was a unique year in many ways, in others it was *very* familiar.

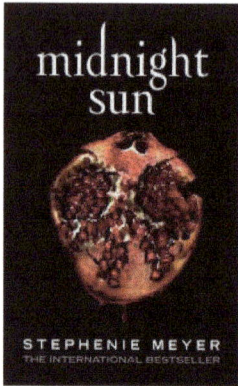

Between them, Rowling and Walliams scored 11 titles in the chart of the top 20 bestselling children's and young adult fiction of 2020. **Stephenie Meyer's** retelling of *Twilight* from Edward Cullen's perspective, *Midnight Sun*, and **Suzanne Collins'** Hunger Games prequel, *The Ballad of Songbirds and Snakes*, hit shelves last year and earn places in the top 20. These eagerly-anticipated novels helped boost a young adult fiction category that had previously been suffering a downturn in recent years.

Despite strong sales, the young adult genre and children's sector as a whole still faces challenges — in particular how to engage older age groups. To a certain extent this challenge is nothing new. Reading or being read to regularly has traditionally always declined as children grow older.

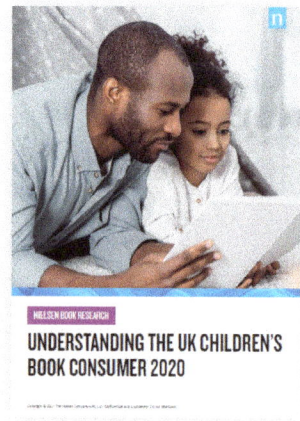

But some findings from our *Impact of COVID-19 on the UK Book Consumers* and *Understanding the UK Children's Book Consumer 2020* reports hint that the pandemic may have accelerated some activity trends that could prove a challenge for children's book publishers and booksellers. In particular, weekly engagement in console gaming, online gaming and app gaming continued to rise last year, while reading books continues to lag behind watching TV, watching YouTube content, and listening to music among 0–17-year-olds as a whole. ⊙

UNDERSTANDING THE UK CHILDREN'S BOOK CONSUMER 2020

UNLOCKING OPPORTUNITY IN THE CHILDREN'S MEDIA INDUSTRY

BY JON MASON

In May 2020 at the height of the first lockdown in the UK, the image of a US police officer kneeling on the neck of George Floyd while in custody flashed around the globe. The combination of his tragic death and the pandemic created a collective conscience.

I, like so many others took to Instagram to post my black square in a show of solidarity. But I felt like a cheat. What was I actually doing that would make any difference? What ACTION could I take?

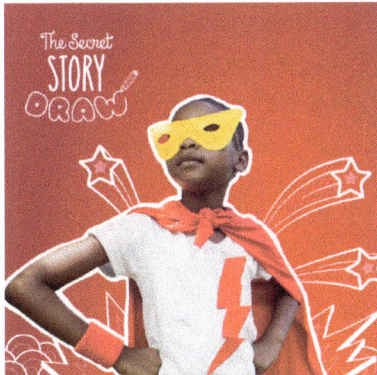

The Secret Story Draw was the idea I came up with.

I'm not a diversity expert and I don't pretend to be, but I was interested. I started reading reports and surveys and I started talking to people in the industry about their experiences. I simply can't thank enough people like, **Laura Henry-Allain** (MBE – Author and Early Years Consultant), **Darren Nartey** (Senior Programmes Acquisitions Executive, ITV) , **Adam Campbell** (Director of Product, Azoomee), **Selom Sunu** (Illustrator and Character Designer), **Nathan Bryon** (Actor and Writer) , **Ere Santos** (Senior Animator, Sony Pictures), **Dino Myers-Lampty** (Founder, The Barber Shop, a Media, Creative and Tech company) and **Joel Airebamen** (Senior Character Animator, Jellyfish Productions) for giving up their time to talk to me and share some of their experiences and also their advice and encouragement to get it off the ground.

JELLYFISH PICTURES

What I'm committed to is getting talented illustrators and animators from under-represented ethnicities into the Children's Media industry. The strange thing is that without the pandemic, I'm not sure I could have made good on my commitment.

The unintended consequence of us all being locked up, was a democratisation of communication; the ability to reach out to important decision makers and stakeholders to help me with the campaign. I didn't have to schlep up to London or Manchester for a 30-minute meeting that had taken weeks to organise, and then weeks of following up.

By sharing my commitment with everyone I know, (and those I didn't), something truly remarkable happened. We ended up with a campaign that is truly unique and incredibly well supported by some of the brightest and the best in the Children's Media industry. The campaign has started to take on a life of its own.

The Secret Story Draw's Premise is simple enough.

THE CHILDREN'S MEDIA CONFERENCE 5–9 JULY 2021 ONLINE We asked some of UK's most renowned children's writers to provide an anonymous story written exclusively for the initiative, with budding animators and illustrators from underrepresented ethnicities invited to bring the stories to life. The Author of each story would remain anonymous until the winners were revealed during the Children's Media Conference Online 2021 in July.

The campaign went live in March, with 12 Children's stories, written by 12 brilliant writers and 12 amazing studios offering up paid internships to the winners.

In eight short months, with literally no money, we've managed to bring together a remarkable group of people. **Ore Oduba** (Presenter), **Keith Chapman** (Founder, Keith Chapman Productions, **Frank Cottrell-Boyce** (author and screenwriter), **Gillian Cross** (author), **Axel Scheffler** (Illustrator), **Jackie Edwards** (Head, Young Audiences Content Fund), **Tom Beattie** (Head of Kids, Tiger Aspect), **Louise Bucknole** (VP Programming Kids, ViacomCBS Networks International) and production companies Aardman, Blue Zoo, Jellyfish Pictures to name only a handful. They've given up their time to write, judge or offer an opportunity. Like I said, it's remarkable. I'm blown away.

I login every day to see who else has submitted. It's the best part of my day and it truly makes me smile. At the time of writing, submissions are more of a trickle than a flood but by the time you read this we will know if the tide had turned.

However, the lack of entries so far raises an uncomfortable truth and points to something I hope campaigns like this will remedy over time. The diversity we seek does not seek us out.

We are quite insular as an industry. The talent we want to find doesn't listen in the channels that we communicate our news, our successes and opportunities in. They're not subscribers to Kidscreen, Bafta or the Children's Media Conference newsletter. Sorry Greg!

They are elsewhere, on channels many of us struggle to keep up with. The studios who can crack the social media code and authentically and credibly communicate with an under-represented audience to build that trust will reap rewards in the long term and the talent will flock to them. We are noisily trying to attract attention to our campaign, but it will take time to build up the trust. Someone said to me - this year should be your pilot, make it happen and next year it will be bigger, your audience will trust it. I hope so.

I'm also not ignorant to the myriad of reasons talent from under-represented communities do not seek out our industry; a wilful lack of funding or support to teach arts & creativity at primary school level, poor or little career advice in secondary school, geographical location, socio economics, the perceived instability of creative careers and quite frankly a lack of anyone who looks the same as you in the industry.

But it's not all doom and gloom. The positive is that things feel like they are changing, moving, shifting from top to bottom. Much has been reported of the structural changes at large organisations. As I've been on this journey, I've met so many amazing people and smaller organisations who are rooted in the purpose of making the industry we all love more representative of everyone we serve; doing brilliant things in this area from all corners of the creative spectrum. There is a world of it. Someone should really try and join it all up! Now that would be a thing.

This year's theme for the Children's Media Yearbook is "Together" and what is at the heart of our initiative is a chance for us all to move together in a spirit of optimism and opportunity - opportunity for everyone. The talent we hope to discover as the campaign rolls out, the opportunity for studios to be part of practical solution and conversation about diversity in this industry, and the optimism and opportunity for all of us to work with and discover new talent and stories to enrich the industry we all love and enjoy.

My hope is for the campaign to be a success and for me to be writing in here again next year, sharing with all of you the success stories from this campaign whilst we're getting ready to announce the winners for the second year.

TOM BROWN'S SCHOOL DAYS

There was no greater change to children's lives than the loss of their school days. Public Service Broadcasters provided a lesson in home schooling to ensure the least disruption to education possible when schools shut down.

BITESIZE: LOCKDOWN LEARNING

HELEN FOULKES

When the country went into a third national lockdown in early January 2021 and schools were closed again to the majority of students, it quickly became apparent that the BBC, once again, needed to do something to help parents, teachers and children.

BBC Director-General **Tim Davie** and Chief Content Officer **Charlotte Moore** challenged the BBC Education team to deliver a new service in under a week. This was a momentous task which couldn't have happened without departments across the BBC coming together. Working closely with colleagues in BBC Two, CBBC, BBC Red Button, BBC iPlayer and the BBC Homepage, the biggest education offer in BBC history was launched just a few days later.

Lockdown Learning brought together hundreds of educational resources on TV, online and social media to help pupils of all ages learn at home. Securing the TV broadcast slots was particularly important to support the almost one million learners without good quality internet access at home.

On TV, we were able to repurpose some of the Bitesize Daily content we had created for the first lockdown back in Spring 2020 and, working closely with colleagues across the BBC, we found a range of new supplementary content that perfectly matched the school curriculum. This required some quick work from the Bitesize team to re-license much of the

partner content shared with us during the summer lockdown, and to engage teachers for a list of programming they'd love to refer to in their virtual classrooms.

Every weekday morning during term time, we provided three hours of programming for Primary children on CBBC and two hours for Secondary students every afternoon on BBC Two.

On CBBC, as well as *Bitesize Daily* lessons, content included four brand new *BBC Teach Live Lessons* – normally only broadcast on the BBC Teach website – and other much loved CBBC shows with an educational twist including *Horrible Histories, Operation Ouch* and *Celebrity Supply Teacher*.

Meanwhile, BBC Two catered for secondary students with programming to support the GCSE curriculum including drama adaptations and relevant BBC science, history and factual programmes. And from February, **Mark Wright** fronted a newly commissioned fitness programme called *Workout the Wright Way*, based around the PE curriculum.

All programming was also available on the BBC Red Button and on BBC iPlayer (in a dedicated Lockdown Learning section); and in the Nations, there were Welsh language packages on S4C and educational programming available every morning on BBC Scotland.

With our online content, we had been planning ahead to provide additional content for increasing numbers of students who were having to work from home. We had already collated a series of easy-to-follow Primary maths and English lessons; collections of resources for Years 1-9 including quizzes, videos and activities; and GCSE revision guides for Years 10 and 11. They were all quickly made available to students on the Bitesize website.

And in addition, we used our social media accounts to provide useful updates for parents and teachers on Facebook and Twitter while teenage students could find explainers, support content and light relief on our Instagram and TikTok accounts.

Of course, providing the content was one thing but making sure that people across the UK knew it was there was another job entirely!

But when the BBC really gets behind something it's amazing how quickly everything can happen. We worked quickly and closely with colleagues across Children's and Education and the wider BBC to get the message out to as wide an audience as possible.

We had prominent articles on the BBC homepage; new presentation links recorded around the CBBC programmes; targeted email comms to parents and teachers; and regular updates on a number of the BBC's social media channels. But even more astounding was a press release that was written in just a few hours and issued shortly before the Prime Minister's press conference on January 6th which he referred to during his televised speech; and a TV and radio trail fronted by **Professor Brian Cox**, that was filmed, edited and shown on networks including BBC One and Radio Two inside 48 hours.

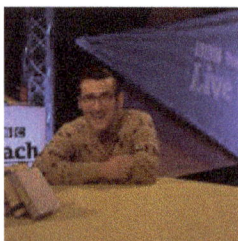

Seeing so many people from various departments across the organisation go above and beyond to achieve the same shared goal was incredible. I'm so proud of everything that the BBC Education department did at that time and so thankful to colleagues across the BBC for their help and support.

But what really matters is the audience. Parents, teachers and students came to the BBC in droves. We launched our Lockdown Learning content on January 11th and on that one day we had 1.6 m unique UK visitors to the BBC Bitesize website; both CBBC and BBC Two saw their slot averages increase considerably; and on BBC iPlayer, *Bitesize Daily* programmes were requested 275K times. Since then, we have continued to see huge numbers coming to our content online, on TV and on the iPlayer. Over the period of the 2021 school closures there was an average of 4.7 million visitors to the Bitesize website each week. And *Bitesize Daily* programmes have been requested over 9 million times from the BBC iPlayer since they were made available in April 2020.

These figures show how important the BBC can be to people in their hour of need and we are thrilled to have supported so many families and teachers across the UK.

Schools are once again opening their doors to pupils which is great to see but that doesn't mean our content will stop. Our support for those needing to isolate during the Summer term will continue online and on TV.

Our new *Bitesize Learning Zone* will deliver three hours of educational programming on CBBC every weekday. Programming will include brand new episodes of *Bitesize Daily* alongside archive content from BBC Education, CBBC and the Natural History Unit. And there will be a wealth of support online where BBC Bitesize will continue to produce This Term's Topics for years 1-9 along with structured Primary lessons in maths and English that match the topics being taught in schools.

I think the BBC has achieved what it set out to do and really made a difference to parents, teachers and children around the country. Only a public service organisation that is committed to Education and has the content and the expertise could deliver something of this scale at such speed.

A PERSONAL VIEW OF BROADCASTING FOR LOCKDOWN

BY KATIE THISTLETON

I credit BBC Bitesize for helping me pass my GCSE's, there's no way I could have done it without those resources and because of that it has definitely got me to where I am now. Ironic really that the BBC's resources have essentially, landed me my job at the BBC.

The BBC has always had excellent educational resources for students and teachers but over the last 12 months the spotlight shone on those resources like never before. The gates to school playgrounds were shut suddenly and parents and carers found themselves scrambling to home-school, teachers were having to educate remotely and a fear started that many children without the support they needed would be left behind and at a disadvantage.

The BBC's educational resources were already stand-out, but we knew something extra was needed to guide people who hadn't navigated through home education before. In the early days of the pandemic and within a matter of weeks the BBC opened the doors on its biggest educational offer in its history. *Bitesize Daily*, comprised of six daily educational shows on BBC iPlayer, daily online lessons for primary and secondary school students and podcasts and educational programming on BBC Four. It was a huge success, visitors to *Bitesize* online averaged 3.8m a week, that's 1.6m more on the same timeframe as 2019.

We all needed all the help and positivity we could get - and *Bitesize Daily* with teachers and celebrities like **Sir David Attenborough** and **Professor Brian Cox** caught the nation's attention. In particular because people needed somewhere to turn. We needed someone to say "I know life is really hard right now but let us help with home-schooling, we're here for you."

I was part of the team who delivered the new *Bitesize Daily* programmes and getting the episodes out as soon as possible to provide something for those parents and kids at home was no mean feat - everyone who worked on it exhausted themselves to make it happen. My phone was ringing non-stop when we launched, you couldn't move for news coverage about the new content.

I also had to polish up on my secondary school maths, English and science too. I made sure to stress to anyone who referred to me as one of the nation's teachers that I was merely the presenter and that *real* teachers and experts were in charge of all the facts. My favourite part of *Bitesize Daily*, which was more my expertise, was our wellbeing strand. It would be themed each day - 'motivation Monday, top tips Tuesday, wellbeing Wednesday' - and mostly involved advice about how to navigate studying and life generally in lockdown, in the most mentally healthy way possible.

Mental health in young people is so important to me. As someone who spends my life doing work mostly in the realm of young people's wellbeing, my first thought when I heard Boris Johnson announce the first lockdown was how on earth the youth were going to survive mentally. I thought of all the issues: loneliness in young people, career pressure, exam stress, social anxiety that I come across regularly when hosting my BBC Radio 1 show and accompanying podcast *'Life Hacks'*.

It was apparent to me immediately that all of these issues could be further exacerbated by the pandemic for those young people. Cancelled exams and ambiguity around results, lack of socialising and hobbies, being at home in potentially damaging environments, delays to furthering education or getting a job or work experience, being locked down in university halls, spending more time on social media, the list goes on. As a team at Radio 1 we focussed on a different aspect of the young person's pandemic experience each week with advice from experts, and released a new series of episodes on BBC Sounds called '*Lockdown Wellbeing*' - 15-minute clips with different experts and advice on the issues that we'd heard first hand young people needed support with.

I'm not sure we've yet seen the full impact of the pandemic on our mental health, and the mental health of our children and young people. On the one hand many have found the pandemic a great time for self-reflection and are coming out stronger. For others the journey is on-going, and coming out of lockdown is presenting another wave of problems, another change which for many might not be so easy.

One thing is for sure, I've never felt prouder to be a small part of the amazing offering there is for our young people here in the UK, whether educating the nation with *Bitesize* or offering advice on *Life Hacks*. I've always championed it to anyone who will listen, but this year the BBC has shone brighter than any other media and has had a long-lasting impact.

Children's media had to step up and make itself known at a time when we all had no choice but to recognise what really matters - and nothing matters more, in my opinion, than the generation who will be our future leaders, creatives and key workers. As one of my favourite quotes goes:

> "we cannot always build the future for our youth, but we can build the youth for our future."
> Franklin D Roosevelt

A WRINKLE IN TIME

The time has come for us to say goodbye to some of those whose talent lit up the lives of young audiences. Thank you for the memories.

JOE RUBY

Writer, Animator and Co-creator, *Scooby- Doo, Where Are You?*

DIANA HINSHELWOOD

—

Joe Ruby and his writing partner Ken Spears met while working at Hanna-Barbera. They originally pitched a cartoon series called *Who's S-S-Scared?* starring a goofy, bongo-playing mongrel named "Too Much". Executive Fred Silverman changed the dog into a Great Dane and renamed him Scooby-Doo and the rest, as they say, is history.

At first, they were worried that *"Scooby-Doo, Where Are You?"* would be a failure when it first aired in 1969. They had no idea that over half a century later Scooby-Doo and his four mystery solving friends would still be delighting children's audiences, having spawned a multimillion-dollar franchise. The latest series, *Scooby-Doo and Guess Who?*, began in 2019.

The mixture of mystery, humour and friendship proved a winning formula for the show – and there was no greater friendship than that of Scooby and his best friend Shaggy. It was one of my favourite childhood programmes and the catch phrases "Scooby-dooby-doo!" and "If it wasn't for those pesky kids…" bring back affectionate memories.

Joe studied art before serving with the US Navy during the Korean War. On his discharge he joined Walt Disney Productions, moving to Hanna-Barbera in 1959, where he first met Ken.

Scooby-Doo remains copyrighted to Hanna-Barbera Productions, and Joe and Ken never felt they were recognised properly for their creation. In 1977, they formed Ruby-Spears Productions and went on the create numerous hit cartoons including *Thundarr The Barbarian* and a reboot of *Alvin And The Chipmunks*. However, the company was eventually taken over by Hanna-Barbera so they ended up back where they started.

Joe Ruby, animator, was born on March 30, 1933. He died of natural causes on August 26, 2020, aged 87 ◔

KEN SPEARS

Writer, Animator and Co-Creator, *Scooby-Doo, Where Are You?*

DIANA HINSHELWOOD

———

"If it wasn't for those pesky kids!"

When *Scooby-Doo, Where Are You?* was first aired on America's CBS network in 1969, Ken Spears and his co-creator, Joe Ruby, were worried it would be a flop. They were up against The Hardy Boys on NBC, and thought they'd have no chance of success.

Instead, *Scooby-Doo* became a hugely successful franchise. Not only were there countless series of the TV show, but feature films, video games, comic books and other spin-offs were created. The most recent TV series, *Scooby-Doo and Guess Who?* began in 2019, half a century after Scooby, Shaggy, Daphne, Velma and the Time Machine made their first appearance.

Ken and Joe didn't know each other initially, but when both were working for animation studio Hanna Barbera, Joe Barbera put them together as a writing team despite the fact that Ken was actually a sound editor.

After 8 years of teamwork on various H-B shows, they came up with an idea for a gentler character to counter the growing violence that was appearing in cartoons. Their idea featured a group of mystery solving friends and their goofy dog, originally called "Too Much" and more of a mongrel. The show went through various versions before Executive Frank Silverman hit on making the dog a Great Dane, though the gentle, goofiness, lop-sided grin and unexpected bravery in the face of danger was kept. The idea for the name came from Frank Sinatra's "doo-be-doo-be-doo" scat singing at the end of his No 1 hit Strangers in the Night.

Scooby-Doo and his friends have delighted generations of children with their mystery-solving antics and are still doing so today. Certainly, it was a highlight of my childhood, and Scooby (as his friends like to call him) is an enduring icon. Ken Spears and his partner, Joe Ruby will always be remembered for their loveable creation, as Scooby-Doo will always be remembered with affection by children the world over.

Scooby-dooby-doo!

Ken Spears, writer and animator, was born on March 12, 1938. He died of complications related to Lewy body dementia on November 6, 2020, aged 82 ◔

ADELE ROSE
Creator of Byker Grove and Scriptwriter

DIANA HINSHELWOOD

Adele Rose was a prolific scriptwriter who created the BBC Children's Drama, *Byker Grove*, which was commissioned by Anna Home, then Head of BBC Children's, in 1988. Set in Newcastle, it starred two unknown child actors, **Anthony McPartlin** and **Declan Donnelly**, and followed the adventures of a group of teenagers finding their way. It was aimed at an older teen and young adult audience, and tackled controversial subjects such as drugs, teen pregnancy and homophobia.

Adele was also the first female script writer on *Coronation Street*, and won a BAFTA for her portrayal of the Street's battleaxes and tough women. She wrote more than 400 episodes between 1961 and 1988, after first joining Granada Television as a secretary. Her other credits include *Heartbeat, Z Cars, Angels* and *Robin's Nest*. She also wrote for *Crossroads* under a pseudonym.

Her husband **Peter Chadwick**, a former newspaper journalist, said of his wife "She had a huge sense of humour which was often quite naughty and wicked."

Those two unknown Geordies from Byker Grove went on to become **Ant and Dec**, the popular TV presenting duo and patrons of Children's Media Foundation. They paid tribute on Twitter, writing: "We are very sad to hear of the passing of Adele Rose, the creator of #BykerGrove. She was an incredible lady and a wonderful writer.

"We will always be grateful for what she did for us and the north-east. Thankyou Adele, and rest in peace."

Adele Rose, Scriptwriter, was born on 8th December 1933 and died of pneumonia on 28th December 2020 aged 87. ◑

JUDITH KERR
Author and Illustrator

DIANA HINSHELWOOD

—

Judith Kerr, one of Britain's most successful children's authors, died in May 2019 aged 95. She was still producing stories and illustrations into her 90s.

Judith was best known for the classic children's book, *The Tiger Who Came to Tea*, and also for *Mog*, a series of picture books of a cat. She was a skilled illustrator with a dry sense of humour and an economic way with words. She once said she never put anything into words that children could work out from the pictures: "it was a waste of energy for children learning to read to spend time to decipher the words only to discover it was something they already knew."

In London, she learnt English, trained as a secretary, worked for the Red Cross during the war and later won a scholarship to the Central School of Arts and Crafts. She became an art teacher, and eventually a BBC scriptwriter until motherhood kept her at home with two small

children. *The Tiger Who Came To Tea* was written after she told them surreal stories to liven up the dull routine of a walk and tea. She eventually added illustrations to make the book, which was first published in 1968 and has never been out of print. Mog was created when her son complained that the books from which he was learning to read were too boring.

She had an ability to see the world from a child's perspective, which is why she will be remembered as one of the most successful and well-loved children's authors.

Judith Kerr, Author and Illustrator, was born on 14th June 1923 and died on 22nd May 2019 aged 95.

SAM MCBRATNEY
Children's Author

BY CECILIA WEISS

—

'I love you right up to the moon'

Writer Sam McBratney, author of the iconic picture book, *Guess How Much I Love You*, died on 18 September 2020.

Sam McBratney was born in Belfast on 1 March 1943. He spent his post-war childhood 'in short trousers and Fair isle jumpers', before going to the local grammar school and then to Trinity College, Dublin, to study History and Political Sciences.

He became a teacher of history and English at a further education college, grammar school and primary school. He also turned began writing children's stories. His first book, *Mark Time,* was published in 1976. Set during the Troubles in Northern Ireland, it featured rival gangs of preteen boys, one Catholic, one Protestant.

He recalls his editor at Walker Books saying to him one day, 'why don't you write a picture book, Sam?' Overriding his protests, she told him that, whilst they had access to highly-talented illustrators, they did not have people who can write a powerful story using hardly any words at all. 'It looks as though it should be easy,' she had said, 'but it's not easy.'

His editor was right, it wasn't easy. He described the new experience, over six months, having every word fighting for its existence in the finished text. "First: yes, in the beginning is the word. The words are simple, direct and true. The words came first."

The result was about 400 words in which Little Nutbrown Hare and his father, Big Nutbrown Hare, try to outdo other in expressing who loves the other more. Next came the gentle illustrations by Anita Jeram. And *Guess How Much I Love You* became an international best-seller, selling more than 50 million copies worldwide, and translated into 57 languages.

His next book, *Will You Be My Friend*, was released on 29th September 2020. Eleven days after he had passed away.

His publisher paid tribute to him: "Sam faced everything in life, and death, with such great, good grace and humour. He always smiled out at the world, and I feel so lucky to have felt the warmth of his smile."

He is remembered by his wife of 56 years, Maralyn, his three children and six grandchildren. And also, by generations of readers whose hearts and minds he touched with his books.

Sam McBratney 1 March 1943 – 18 September 2020

JAMES NASH
Children's Author and Illustrator

BY CECILIA WEISS

—

James Nash was the author and illustrator of the beautiful children's book, 'The Winter Wild: Long Tails and Lantern Light'. On 4 August last year he was tragically murdered.

He was born and grew up in Dorset. As an adult he had a successful career in the aerospace industry, trained as a teacher, and then followed his dream to become an artist, writer and poet. He worked as a journalist, publishing articles in newspapers and magazines. He ran writing workshops and acted as a literary host at festivals across the country. His first book, The Winter Wild: Long Tails and Lantern Light, was published in 2016. He then wrote, 'The Legends of Holly Tree: Henry and the Major'.

He is remembered by all who knew him for his creativity, artistic talent, writing skills. And, above all, for his kindness.

The Test Valley Arts Foundation paid him this tribute: "James was a talented artist and writer. He was charming, soft spoken and completely genuine. He captivated the audiences he worked with and young people adored him."

Using James's words from Twitter, he said that he had set up an "art studio from his home and between teaching art classes, he spent time writing and illustrating and repairing an old tractor gifted to Enham Trust during the war." He lived his life as he wanted, acknowledged by all for his creativity and kind-heartedness.

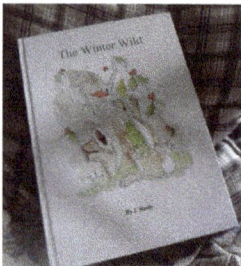

The potential and career of this talented writer and illustrator was tragically stolen from him on that day last year. Our thoughts remain with his wife, mother, father, sister and many friends. We end this article with his mother's words:

"We have lost a beautiful, talented son and brother and I know all who knew him would say he was the kindest, most caring person."

James Nash 12 February 1978 – 4 August 2020

TERRY JONES

LEWIS RUDD

—

Terry Jones started his television career as a writer for mainstream comedy shows, and after all the success of the Python years, became a prolific author of children's books. And had that been his only contribution to the lives of children – he would have warranted a mention in the Children's Media Yearbook.

However, not everyone will be aware that there is another qualification. His career as an on-screen performer began in the ITV children's sketch show *Do Not Adjust Your Set,* which I initiated as Head of Children's Programmes at Rediffusion in 1967.

The idea of making the programme was suggested by the success of the adult sketch show *At Last The 1948 Show,* and I had the sense to enrol as producer, Humphrey Barclay, then responsible for the adult radio comedy *I'm Sorry I'll Read That Again.* He put together the team of five - three of them writer-performers, **Terry Jones** and **Michael Palin** (who had become a duo at Oxford) and **Eric Idle** from the Cambridge Footlights, together with **David Jason** and **Denise Coffey.**

The attraction for the three writers was the chance to emerge from the shadows of the writers' room and actually appear on television. None of them had, so far as I knew, any particular ambition to be involved in children's programmes. Humphrey, too, was attracted principally by the move to TV. We were all in fact feeling our way. I had only recently moved to children's programmes from being a current affairs producer.

The challenge to Terry and the others as writers and performers was to work out the parameters of what was likely to work for children, making a mainly studio-based show as visual as possible, and what areas would appeal. Somebody (possibly Terry) decided that our equivalent of sex jokes would be food jokes.

While on the whole the programme was a delight to be involved in, I found myself from

time to time having to act as censor. It will not surprise anyone who knew Terry at all that he was the one who would dig his heels in when a change was suggested, whereas Michael, already preparing for his role as the nicest man in Britain, would pour oil on troubled waters and suggest a compromise. I have dim memories of a particular dispute over euphemisms for going to the lavatory, but half a century has blotted out what the resolution was!

Terry and Michael were also the writers of the five-minute filmed serial in the programme, *Captain Fantastic*, performed by David and Denise, and very generously continued to be involved when I filched it as a boost to the newly launched magazine programme *Magpie*.

Even after the success of *Monty Python* Terry remained a loyal friend, obligingly making the trek to Birmingham in the 1980s to appear on Central's early morning *Saturday Show* for me.

YOU DID IT!

Children's Media Yearbook 2021 contributors

JOHN CARR

John Carr is an expert on internet safety and was a Founding Director of the British Internet Watch Foundation (1996). He holds a variety of posts concerning internet safety for children such as Technical Adviser, ECPAT International and Secretary, Children's Charities' Coalition on Internet Safety, Member of the Academic Advisory Network of the Chief Constable of Norfolk, the national lead on online child sexual exploitation for the British police, Member of the Advisory Panel on Children's Viewing of the British Board of Film Classification. He is also a Visiting Senior Fellow, London School of Economics and Political Science.

CAROLINE CASSON

Senior Market Research Manager, Ofcom, Caroline has worked in the Market Research team at Ofcom for over seven years and has experience managing both quantitative and qualitative research projects. She is a core member of Ofcom's Media Literacy research team and leads Ofcom's longitudinal tracking survey into children's use, understanding and attitudes of media. Caroline is passionate about this topic and keen to share Ofcom's research to support the work of government, organisations and agencies. Caroline joined Ofcom in 2005 having previously worked in both government and media companies for over ten years prior.

GREG CHILDS

Greg Childs worked for over 25 years at the BBC, mainly as a director, producer and executive producer of children's programmes. He created the first children's BBC websites and, as Head of Children's Digital, developed and launched the children's channels CBBC and CBeebies. Greg left the BBC in 2004 and subsequently advised producers on digital, interactive, and cross-platform strategies; and broadcasters on channel launches, digital futures and management support. He was in the launch team for Teachers TV and the CITV Channel in the UK, and was advisor to the Al Jazeera Children's Channel for three years consulting with the European Broadcasting Union on their Children's and Youth strategy. Greg has been Editorial Director of the Children's Media Conference for the last fifteen years. He is also one the Heads of Studies at the German Akademie Fur Kindermedien and is Director of the audience advocacy body – the Children's Media Foundation.

SARAH DOYLE

Sarah joined Kids Industries having gained a First-Class Honours Degree in Animation from the University for the Creative Arts. Sarah has worked as a digital designer for over 5 years and is passionately interested in game design, digital painting, player behaviour and storytelling. She has a particular interest in the design of games and apps for children and has driven the design for a wide variety of much loved branded digital products including work on the multi award winning Warrior Cats platform for Coolabi, Amazing Planet for WWF and a raft of others for clients as diverse as Universal and Encantos. She has played a part in the digital lives of many of the most loved of today's children's characters including Peppa, Paw Patrol, TMNT and SpongeBob. Sarah has voluntarily produced three sessions over the past two years for the Children's Media Conference Inclusivity Now strand. In 2020 she produced two video sessions for Hopster and Inclusive Minds on 'Intentional Inclusion in Children's Books' and Preschool and Prejudice - 'Is Kids TV Making Your Child Prejudiced?' This year she is currently working on another session on Manga and Inclusivity. Sarah has a passion for illustration and character art..

JACKIE EDWARDS

Jackie is Head of the BFI Young Audiences Content Fund, and is responsible for the successful implementation of this game changing UK Government initiative to stimulate the provision of public service content for audiences of 0-18, Jackie joined the BFI from BBC Children's where she had been the Head of Acquisitions and Independent Animation, responsible for pre-buying and acquiring live-action and animated programming for CBeebies, CBBC and iPlayer. She joined the BBC in 2008 as Content Manager and Executive Producer. Prior to the BBC Jackie was an award winning producer in the Independent Sector. A passionate advocate for public service content, Jackie is currently living her dream job!.

LOTTE ELWELL

Lotte Elwell started her career at BBC Children's where she worked for 12 years working her way up from runner to Series Producer. After leaving the BBC, she freelanced as a director on series such as Teletubbies, My World Kitchen, My Pet and Me and the Peppa Pig Cinema experience before joining forces with Katie Simmons and setting up independent company - King Banana TV to produce their own series – Yakka Dee! for CBeebies. The series was inspired by observing her daughter develop her speech and realising that many parents had concerns about their children's speech development and needed resources to help. Yakka Dee! has been a global success and now shows round the world and has over 250 million views on YouTube. King Banana make successful, high quality, audience-led series for global broadcasters and are currently working with Boom Kids on 'Meet the Experts' – a live action series they created for Milkshake. The company aims to empower children through content that inspires curiosity, delights and surprises and believes in putting as many different children on screen as possible. King Banana is a female-led company that pushes for a flexible workforce to allow parents to return to work. We are passionate about encouraging new talent from diverse backgrounds both in front and behind the camera!

HELEN FOULKES

Helen Foulkes is Head of BBC Education overseeing BBC Bitesize, BBC Teach, BBC Food and the BBC's educational campaigns. Our aim is to 'Transform lives through Education'. BBC Bitesize is the most used educational website in the UK, which is used by 80% of secondary school students; BBC Teach supports teachers with world class, curriculum linked content for use in the classroom; and education campaigns that address a societal or educational deficit, from Ten Pieces and Super Movers to BBC micro:bit. Prior to working in BBC Education Helen has a wide range of Television Executive Producer credits including Points of View, Country Tracks, See Hear and To Buy or Not to Buy. Before becoming an executive she worked across a multitude of BBC brands such as Holiday, Homefront and What Not to Wear.

Maxine Fox

As Managing Director of Giraffe Insights, an international research agency, specialising in youth, kids and family insight, Maxine leads a dedicated team working across a number of disciplines. With over a decade working in research, she has become an industry recognised specialist in speaking to kids, young people and families to elicit the greatest insights for brands.

DIANA HINSHELWOOD

Diana has worked in Children's Media for over 30 years on well-known Children's programmes such as "Record Breakers" "Grange Hill" "Going Live" and "Playdays". She joined CBeebies as an On-Air producer at the launch of the channel in 2002, and in 2006 collaborated with Children's Radio to create and launch CBeebies Radio. On leaving the BBC, Diana worked on "Lazytown", "Sarah and Duck" and "The Fluffy Club" and developed TV and Radio projects. She also produced for digital platforms such as Espresso Education (Now Discovery) and Open University, and is currently a freelance development producer and scriptwriter, winning 2 commissions from CBeebies Radio and option agreements for animations.Diana is the Newsletter Editor of the Children's Media Foundation Newsletter, and a member of the CMF Executive Group.

ANNA HOME OBE

Anna began working for the BBC in 1960 and started working in the children's department in 1964. She has won many accolades, including a BAFTA Lifetime Achievement award. Anna was the first Chair of the BAFTA Children's Committee, and has chaired both the EBU Children's and Youth Working Group and the Prix Jeunesse International Advisory Board. She was also the Chair of the Save The Kids' TV Campaign Executive Committee and the Showcomotion children's media conference.She now chairs the Board of the Children's Media Conference and the Children's Media Foundation, and is a Board member of Screen South.

SALLYANN KEIZER

BAFTA and International Emmy award-winning Sallyann Keizer, is passionate about children, mental health and dogs! Ideally all mixed together in her latest media offering, bow-wowza.com. A trained journalist, she set up independent production company Sixth Sense Media in 2000, to give young people a voice and to empower, inspire, and entertain children globally. Sixth Sense has over the past two decades delivered hundreds of episodes of children's shows to global broadcasters and Sallyann is a dedicated advocate for mental health and DEI, and speaks on these topics on the world stage.

BARONESS BEEBAN KIDRON OBE

Baroness Beeban Kidron OBE is a Crossbench Peer in the House of Lords and Chair of 5Rights Foundation. After 30 years as an award-winning film director, Kidron was appointed to the House of Lords as a Crossbench Peer. In Parliament, Kidron is a strong advocate for digital regulation and accountability; most particularly in relation to children under the age of 18. In 2018, Kidron introduced 'the Age Appropriate Design Code' as an amendment to the Data Protection Act 2018, and is co-founder of the All-Party Parliamentary Group for Digital Regulation and Responsibility. Baroness Kidron is the Founder and Chair of 5Rights Foundation, a charity whose mission is to build the digital world children and young people deserve. 5Rights recently supported the UN Committee on the Rights of the Child in drafting general comment number 25 on the relevance of children's rights to the digital environment (formally adopted March 2021). Baroness Kidron sits on various Boards, including UNESCO Broadband Commission; Global Council on Extended Intelligence; University of Oxford's Institute of Ethics in AI; Born in Bradford Digital Makers Programme and she Chairs 5Rights Foundation's Digital Futures Commission.

JAYNE KIRKHAM

Writer, Secretary to the All-Party Parliamentary Group on Children's Media and the Arts Jayne has developed and written for most formats: from animation to radio to app to picture book to live action feature for all ages. Original commissions include poetry and short stories to help young people have fun in the wider world. Jayne is a Director of the Children's Media Foundation, for whom she acts as political liaison. In 2011 she formed the All-Party Parliamentary Group for Children's Media and the Arts and works closely with its co-chairs Baroness Floella Benjamin and Julie Elliott MP.

SONIA LIVINGSTONE

Sonia Livingstone DPhil (Oxon), OBE, FBA, FBPS, FAcSS, FRSA, is a professor in the Department of Media and Communications at the London School of Economics and Political Science. She has published 20 books on media audiences, especially children and young people's risks and opportunities, media literacy and rights in the digital environment. Her new book is "Parenting for a Digital Future: How hopes and fears about technology shape children's lives" (Oxford University Press, with Alicia Blum-Ross). She is currently leading the Digital Futures Commission with the 5Rights Foundation.

HELEN LOCKETT

Helen is Research Manager at Discovery, and a core member of The Hub, Discovery's kids and youth offering. She is passionate about youth research, with experience covering a broad range of sectors including media, finance, education and more. Helen combines her extensive quantitative experience with qualitative insights, to deep dive into what kids are doing and why. She uses a variety of research techniques to gain practical insights, helping brands to understand young people and how to engage with them.

JON MASON

Founder/MD – Jollywise & Secret Story Draw Campaign Champion. Jon Mason has worked in digital media production for over 20 years. Following an early career as a creative producer at Walt Disney he founded Jollywise a creative digital studio. Their work for clients like Disney, BBC, PBS, DreamWorks and Sesame workshop has been dedicated to producing brilliant, thoughtful digital content that connects with children of all ages.

GARY POPE

Gary began his career as a school teacher leading an English department before becoming a learning designer for a change management consultancy. He co-founded Kids Industries in 1999 and today leads the agency as CEO to find answers to the most challenging problems in the family market. With a number of industry accolades under his belt, Gary has created and executed award-winning marketing campaigns for numerous FMCG brands, hotels, global learning programmes, theme parks, private island destinations and globally recognised, best-in-class digital products. He is the recipient of a BAFTA for the Co-creation of the Disney Channel Kids Awards, two Institute of Practitioners in Advertising Special Awards for Strategy (Glaxosmithkline and Aquafresh) and a Webby award for a campaign with Peppa Pig. A firm believer in furthering education and increasing marketing campaign success rates, Gary is an advisor to The Children's Media Conference and a guest lecturer at multiple academic institutions - including Bauhaus and Oxford Universities. He is also regularly called upon by the national and trade press to comment on industry news within the global family market press. Gary maintains his interest in education as a school governor, is dad to Daisy and Laurence and is a proud LEGO collector.

KRUKAE POTHONG

Dr Kruakae Pothong is a Researcher at 5Rights and visiting research fellow in the Department of Media and Communications at London School of Economics and Political Science. Her current research focuses on child-centred design of digital services. Her broader research interests span the areas of human-computer interaction, digital ethics, data protection, Internet and other related policies. She specialises in designing social-technical research, using deliberative methods to elicit human values and expectations of technological advances, such as the Internet of Things (IoT) and distributed ledgers.

LEWIS RUDD, MBE

Lewis Rudd M.B.E. was for over thirty years an executive producer or head of department for children's programmes in a number of different ITV companies. His programmes included 'Do Not Adjust Your Set' (involving four of the subsequent Monty Python team, as well as David Jason), 'Magpie', 'Rainbow', 'The Sooty Show', 'Worzel Gummidge', 'Murphy's Mob', 'Emu's World', 'Woof', 'Your Mother Wouldn't Like It', 'Press Gang', 'Wise Up', and 'Goodnight Mister Tom'. He also served as Executive Producer of the European Broadcasting Union Children's Drama Exchange, and was involved in international co-productions with Swedish Television·

and ABC Australia. He has been a member of the British Board of Film Classification's panel on Children's Viewing, the Children's Media Foundation Executive Group, and a director of the Voice of the Listener and Viewer. Lewis's recollections of his life in Broadcasting were published as "Not Just About Managing" in 2018.

MARCUS RYDER

Marcus Ryder is an award-winning executive producer at Caixin Global, China's leading financial publication. He is a visiting professor in media diversity at Birmingham City University and was a core member of the executive committee to launch the Sir Lenny Henry Centre for Media Diversity. He has worked in television for more than 25 years. For eight years he oversaw BBC Scotland's current affairs documentaries where he formulated his ideas on the importance of diverse representation championing communities as opposed to simply increasing the representation of different types of individuals.

JULIAN SCOTT

Julian Scott is a BAFTA-nominated Executive Producer. He has been developing, financing and co-producing feature films and television in the international arena for over 25 years. As animation consultant for Film London, his focus is on generating inward investment for London's

animation studios, by finding partners outside the UK seeking creative and financial soulmates and advising on the UK animation tax credits. Other areas of his work include tackling skills and creative gaps in the animation industry and lobbying to get proper recognition for animation in the UK creative sector and advising studios on business and creative development..

NIKKI STEARMAN

Nikki is a Senior Game Designer at Dubit; creating playful and meaningful digital experiences for children. She has worked in children's digital media for over 16 years; first specialising in e-learning and then later in games as a Producer at CBBC. She is a proud owner of a BAFTA for her CBBC game, and most recently a Kidscreen Award for her work on the GoNoodle Games app.

KATIE THISTLETON

After working as a Researcher for CBeebies, Katie made the leap in front of the camera at the start of 2013 after being headhunted to join the CBBC HQ line-up to host 'the bits in between the shows', a role once occupied by the likes of Phillip Schofield and Zoe Ball. Katie hosted CBBC's live continuity for over six years, claiming the title of the longest running presenter to occupy that role, before leaving to

concentrate on her work at Radio 1. After deputising on BBC Radio 1's The Surgery in early 2016, Katie became the show's main anchor before being promoted to the coveted Sunday slot with the new 'Life Hacks' programme. Katie and her co-presenter Vick Hope host the social action show, an appointment which made them the first female double act on BBC Radio 1 in 20 years. The pair alongside experts offer advice on topics ranging from sexual health and bullying to drink and drugs. The pair also host Radio 1's Official Chart First look on Sunday evenings. After becoming a firm favourite, Katie can also be seen (and heard!) at Radio 1's Big Weekend and Radio 1's Teen Awards and regularly deputises for other DJs. Katie regularly covers for Scott Mills on The Official Chart and Adele Roberts on early breakfast. In addition, Katie hosts the weekly 'Life Hacks' podcast with the show's resident Doctor, Radha for BBC Sounds. As a proud Mancunian and radio enthusiast Katie also regularly covers the breakfast show on BBC Radio Manchester as well as the mid-morning and lunchtime shows, further demonstrating her radio skills hosting phone-ins on topics ranging from hard-hitting political debates to more light-hearted chatties, and interviewing MP's, celebrities and local people. Katie is passionate about mental health awareness, she is an ambassador for charities Place2be and YoungMinds and is currently training to be a counsellor. Katie writes a monthly column for Psychologies Magazine about issues regularly faced by twenty-something's. Katie has appeared on The One Show and This Morning, hosting a film for the former about the lasting mental health affects of the Manchester Arena attack on young victims, and appearing on the sofa to offer advice. Katie has been an 'agony aunt' on This Morning's sofa alongside Ruth and Eamonn offering advice to young students receiving exam results. She has also hosted numerous documentaries for the BBC, on topics ranging from anti-depressants to the Kardashians, and recently a series called 'I've Been There' for the teen audience, on topics such as knife crime, cosmetic surgery, anxiety and depression. In May 2021, Katie hosted the audio documentary series Manchester Arena Bomb: Stories of Hope for BBC Sounds. The series saw Katie finding stories of courage, hope and healing as fans, families and those affected by the atrocity rebuild their future four years on. During lockdown in 2020 when schools were closed, Katie was chosen to be the main presenter fronting the Bitesize Daily TV shows for secondary school students, linking between educational content and interviewing teachers. The shows received record-breaking viewing figures. Building on her 'agony aunt' experience, Katie's debut book 'Dear Katie: Real Problems, Real Advice' was released in February 2018 and offers warm yet honest advice on the multitude of struggles the UK's children are facing. Katie is currently writing her second book. A keen book worm herself, Katie also founded and hosted her own show 'The CBBC Book Club' for five years and regularly hosts and judges for book events such as the BBC Young Writers Award, The Lollies for Scholastic and David Walliams' publication events, amongst many more. Considered by many as a safe pair of hands with a calm and engaging presenting style, Katie has hosted a variety of live shows including Hacker's Birthday Bash, a celebration of 30 years of Children's BBC, Hacker's Crackers, Shout Out Saturday and Junior Bake Off: The After Party, as well as CBBC coverage of large events such as Wimbledon and Live from Alder Hey Children's Hospital. Other credits include, Celebrity Mastermind, Celebrity Eggheads, BBC Radio 2, Children in Need, BBC 5Live and BBC Breakfast, where Katie has appeared to talk about children's mental health and sex education.

TOM VAN WAVEREN

Tom van Waveren began his career in animation at Nelvana in 1996 as Director of its London office. In 1999, Tom moved to Copenhagen to head up Egmont Imagination as its President where he was involved in the production of over 100 hours of animation, including Paz, Rex the Runt, Little People and Hamilton Mattress, and the distribution of Lizzie McGuire. Tom started his own company Hoek, Line & Thinker in 2004 and merged his pipeline of projects with CAKE in 2006. Since that date, he has been responsible for scouting, development and the executive production of all CAKE content. Tom has been nominated three times for a daytime Emmy, still waiting for that win, and has been overseeing a development slate of over 20 properties from pre-school to animation for 6-12 years, as well as all CAKE's current productions, which have included over the years, Skunk Fu!, Angelo Rules, Oscar's Oasis, Bottersnikes & Gumbles, Space Chickens in Space, Mush Mush and the Mushables, Mama K's Team 4, and Angry Birds: Summer Madness. Tom has been the CEO and Creative Director at CAKE from 2006 through to April 2021. Apart from that, he is currently a Vice-Chair of Animation in Europe, where he is working to improve support for the European animation industry.

COLIN WARD

Colin is Deputy Director of the Children's Media Foundation and is responsible for the CMF's Executive Group and links with the research community. His long career in children's TV started at Yorkshire Television, working across factual, entertainment and drama formats. He won a Bafta for 'The Scoop' before joining Granada Kids to produce the Bafta-nominated gameshow 'Jungle Run'. Moving to the BBC, he won a second Bafta for the gameshow 'Raven', going on to work as an Executive Producer with CBBC Scotland on a range of entertainment and drama formats. He now combines freelance writing and directing with work as a lecturer in film and television production at the University of York.

CECILIA WEISS

Cecilia has over 20 years' experience in children's television and digital educational media. She worked in BBC Schools TV as PA, director, research, and then became a producer for CBeebies Interactive. After leaving the BBC, she worked on a range of freelance projects, and is currently the editor of iChild, a website providing resources for children.

www.ingramcontent.com/pod-product-compliance
Lightning Source LLC
Chambersburg PA
CBHW051316020426
42333CB00028B/3367